MEG L ___ I

watch
YA
language

Shift your dialogue
from self-judgement
and comparison
to acceptance
and compassion

the kind press

Cover design: Mila Book Covers
Editing: Georgia Jordan
Internal design: Nicola Matthews, Nikki Jane Design

Cataloguing-in-Publication
entry is available from the
National Library Australia.

NATIONAL
LIBRARY
OF AUSTRALIA

ISBN: 978-0-6452626-3-6 paperback
ISBN: 978-0-6452626-4-3

Every time a white butterfly crosses my path, I am reminded of you. I feel your presence often and it ripples through me as a reminder to keep going.

This book not only is a dedication to you, Nan, but to every human who has not been able to feel, express or let go of the past. To every human who still lives in guilt, shame or blame: I see you and I devote this book to you.

I know we didn't often see eye to eye, Nan, but we were never meant to. Your profound teachings of surrender will never be lost on me.

I promise to be a voice not only for myself, but for others who are struggling. I promise to bring to light the things that should be talked about, and never shut down. I share from my heart a voice that can speak for many on how we as humans, in the world we live in today, have the ability to make a choice.

A choice to follow our hearts. A choice to be unashamedly ourselves. Our dialogue, essentially, can be the change that the world needs.

Fly high, Nan. You are always with me.

With so much love.

CONTENTS

INTRODUCTORY MESSAGE

Writing this book is my healing. This is my promise to myself to do what I was intended to do. This is my voice, this is my heart, and this is my soul.

I am always open to being taught. I will always be the practitioner and student. I aim to be open, teachable and fluid throughout the rest of my life.

I am a passionate human whose intention and heartfelt desire is to change the world.

I am limitless. And so are you.

To land here, I have had twenty-eight years of lived experience with eating disorders, bulimia, anorexia, mental health struggles, body dysmorphia, self-harm and depression. I only speak from my own knowledge and share with honesty, the best I can, the tools from others I have picked up along the way.

I don't know enough to be right. I don't think any of us do, because we are constantly changing, growing and learning. However, I hope this book might fill some gaps, answer a few questions, and above all, give you permission to start to put yourself first. For the only thing we can do is be ourselves. If others around you need help and you are caught in a battle of trying to fix them, change them or direct them in a new way, from experience and with a gentle wish, I urge you to pause and put that energy back into yourself.

If there is one thing I have learnt along the way and hope to share in the guts of this book, it is to *put yourself first*. Your showing up, your journey to your best self, your love, compassion and kindness to yourself is your magnet and mirror to those who are around you … especially your kids. When you give back to you, they see YOU step up and that has a ripple effect.

My promise to you is honesty, vulnerability, and a complete messy and undeniably uncomfortable truth. My intention for you, the reader, is to experience this book with a sense of openness, acceptance that my values may not line up with your own, and a childlike curiosity of *What would happen if I allowed myself to feel?*

I have two incredible humans, Robbie and Ian, who are my chosen parents, and my 'second mother' Dorte Parker; I am so thankful and filled with love for you all. These guys showered me with love as any parents would.

We only know what we know. Please remember throughout this book that this is *my experience* through the eyes of someone who never thought they were enough.

I am going to lay it all out on the table—the awkward, the uncomfortable, the messy, the shitty, and the stuff we don't want to talk about. I'm not kidding.

If I haven't lost you, and already you feel discomfort—great! I encourage you to hold on, buckle up and get ready to do the work. I am constantly faced with 'the work', but I would rather be doing the work than staying comfortable. We all know we have to feel fear to grow.

I encourage you to do the same.

If you are in a rut with your dialogue, thoughts and behaviours, and decide you can't keep going on the way you are, then this is the right book for you.

I ask you to lean in, surrender, and trust you are exactly where you need to be.

You are here for a reason.

And so am I.

It's time to 'watch ya language' and shift your self-talk for good!

Megs x

A SPECIAL THANK YOU

I am likely to miss some of you, but know that every single person I have touched base with in my life has been a part of this incredible journey, and I am so grateful for you and what I have learnt from you, or with you.

To my mum and dad: you both know the reality of my ride from day one, and it is with utmost compassion that I hold so much respect, love and appreciation for your support, guidance and love. You both have endured so much and I hope you know that what you both offered to me was absolutely perfect; it was exactly the way it was meant to be. Thank you and I love you.

Meags Soley ... my soul sister, my best mate, the sunflower in my life that just keeps on helping me step up and shine brighter. Your energy is contagious and addictive, and I have been so lucky to share this journey with you and see you embrace your heart space and give back to so many others. You are such a gift to the world.

Melinda Carbis-Reilly. You are one of the most vulnerable,

open, loving and caring humans I have ever met. I am grateful for our friendship, our hugs and our boob and butt squeezes. Never ever a fan of those earrings though. I am so proud of the woman you are and the message you share with the world. It's so very needed.

To every single one of my family, friends, clients, boyfriends, lovers and students, you all are still teaching me so much and I am beyond humbled from your support, love and trust.

And to the teachers, mentors and everyone else who supported me through the darkest days of my eating disorder: seeing someone you love move through this disease is heartbreaking, and you were there when I needed love the most. Thank you.

To my movement culture, Infuse Health, The Movement Collective, Soisci Porchetta and Redhead Wellness: you all helped me see movement from a place of love, allowing me to embrace and embody the idea of moving to *feel good*, not exercising to *punish*. I have never played so much in my life and it is not going to stop now.

To my fur baby, Lilly. If you are on my YouTube (Meg Linton) or Instagram (@watch.ya.language), you will see that she loves to take the centre of attention. For your ever-forgiving, unconditional love, I adore you.

Tim. You taught me that anything I desired was attainable. You showed me love that reflected where I was, and it blew my mind. I knew I had finally broken through the barriers of unworthiness, doubt and not being enough when I met you. We went there. The places we explored, clothed or not, the energy we felt, the conversations we had, and the moments that were shared were the most incredible, alive and real experiences I have ever allowed myself to feel. I have so much love and gratitude for the time we spent together. You will always hold such a space in my heart.

To Kirsty Seward and Cathy Feenan, my mates that have helped me show up in ways I never thought possible. I continually count my lucky stars that I am able to collaborate with you both in our retreats, and am blessed for our solid friendship. I stand by and honour your work in the world greatly and know you are both here to do amazing things for the world.

To Michael O'Sullivan for your support, love and friendship. You have a heart of gold and I am so grateful to you for helping me stick to my dreams and desires, and to never ever lose sight of them. I love our Monday catch-ups of goal setting, vision planning and acai bowls.

My biggest teacher, Nan. You taught me the biggest lesson that I will ever learn: to always follow my heart, to surrender, to forgive and to let go. You are always in my heart and I thank you for the consistent reminder of your presence each time white butterflies surround me when I am on the right track.

I devote this book to you.

VIBRATIONS IN THE HEART

My nan passed before I completed this book. So, thank you, Nan, for all you taught me, and most importantly, for letting go. You taught me the biggest lesson I will ever learn. Surrender.

This book is all about our heart. It is our teacher, our voice. It has so many different levels of singing, however we rarely let ourselves access the full range.

This is what this book is about. The teaching here is life changing.

When we can understand our heart, rather than run from or numb the ever-changing emotions (vibrations), we can start to learn to sit with them, experience them and move with them in the moment ... rather than push them down. This is how we start to learn how to feel, to heal.

I'm not going to lie. This book has had many different attempts, so many forced starts and stagnations, and a long time waiting for me to be ready.

So, here I am. Undeniably, I have learnt much from writing

these words and recounting these stories. The writing process presented many opportunities to dive deep into my experiences. It forced me to face the music, to be triggered by my own words, and of course, say thank you, show up, and do the work.

The world situation at the time of writing, 2022, is throwing us some moments that ask us to show up, speak our truth, and come back to humanity as one.

The Dalai Lama speaks of humans as being gentle and compassionate—that is our natural state. To judge another, to claim we are right over another, to blame another for their actions and to think that we are better than another is not the way forward. Whatever actions humans are taking in this world are coming from a place of fear and pain.

Unresolved trauma in the body will come out when we are triggered in our environment. Things such as lockdowns and stay-at-home orders can bring to the surface any childhood trauma or emotions that we have spent most of our lives numbing or running from. The times we are in are forcing society to face emotions some of us have been unwilling to feel and this is creating what some may describe as chaos on a large scale.

In the Western world, it seems common to push emotion down and 'soldier on'—to keep a brave front and be strong, even if it doesn't feel right.

Nothing suppressed will ever go away. In fact, the emotion 'lifts weights and trains every day', gaining momentum until it pops up in your mind when you least expect it. This is not fun. I have first-hand experience of witnessing emotions that had been suppressed for many, many years.

If I can share any advice for the times in which we live—do your best to see the person you are judging as a person who is suffering and in pain. The only reason people choose actions that we don't understand is that there is something under layers that has not been healed. Humans have a common desire to be happy and to not suffer. Emotional pain and trauma not felt for some time manifests in the body and if we don't have the tools to deal with it when we are triggered, it can come across as stupidity, aggression and resentment.

Love is the only way forward and compassion is our natural state. Be the light.

> Be the light you wish to see in the world.
> — Unknown

Your ability to watch ya language will give permission for those around you to do the same.

You may identify with one or some of the people listed below, or you may know people like them:

- Women and men enduring a constant battle with the noisy voice inside our head
- Teens trapped in the belief of *I'll be better when* and *I'm not enough*
- Mums trying to do their best for their kids or trying to fix them, but remaining in a constant battle with their own bodies
- Everyone who knows there is another way, but stays in the safe zone because that is all they know, and continues to experience suffering
- The adult who has had enough of the shitty language they have been talking to themselves in for most of their lives, but is unsure how to change it
- The people pleaser who constantly puts others first and

doesn't know how to fill their own cup
- And … last but maybe not least, the perfectionist who is always searching for more

Nothing works if you don't look after yourself first. It's up to *you* which garden you choose to water.

A PERSONAL NOTE

As I neared completion of this book, so much became clear to me. I became a new human—completely different from who I was not so long ago. I used to pride myself on my status, attachments, achievements and what I had. I used to compare myself to those around me and put myself (or others) on a pedestal, constantly thinking one was better than another.

I would strive to be right. I would fight for the last word and I would blame everything and everyone around me for life not going the way I had planned. I was in a constant struggle with a label, a definition or another step up the ladder.

Danish philosopher Søren Kierkegaard said: 'Once you label me, you negate me.'

I have learnt that we are not just a body. We are a soul living a human experience. As such, what we have, what we own, how we look and how we define ourselves is ultimately a whole load of BS. We will all grow old, we will all lose our physical form and get wrinkles, have problems pooping, and need assistance feeding ourselves at some point. The more we accept and lean into that, the easier the acceptance of our true selves becomes.

Having realised this, it has now become my practice to treat everyone around me as an equal—another human who ultimately is also looking for love, compassion and happiness, just like me or you. I also don't get this right all the time, and fuck it up more often than not, but I do have much more awareness now. It is no longer my 'learnt response' to judge and compare myself or others; now I choose compassion and kindness instead.

This, of course, is still largely a practice. I still judge, I still compare and I still get caught up in my ego when I am out of alignment and let fear and doubt take over from the guidance of God. It is when we surrender control to something higher—be that God, Source, a divine spirit, our highest self or whatever else we choose it to be—that we let go of how we *think* things should be, and allow ourselves to flow and receive the signs of spiritual guidance, love and fluidity that guide us to our natural, effortless state.

We are about to uncover how you can watch ya language to start to step up, show up and move towards the highest, vibrant and energetic self that you are here to be.

Remember: you have a choice. That choice is right now. No ifs, no buts. No excuses for why things are the way they are, such as *I was born this way* or *It's in my family*. This moment is a brand-new opportunity to make a choice.

The moment is going to be what it is ...

unpleasant	nasty	hurtful	painful
happy	grateful	shameful	embarrassing
joyful	frustrating	dark	heavy
playful	sad	vibrant	

They are all moments. It's up to you how you respond (or react) to them. If you're ready … let's dive in.

But before we get stuck in, there are a few things you need to know.

This is not just another self-help book to sit on your shelf. If you are all in, get ready for the ride. #watchyalanguage.

This is not a book about eating disorders, but I do believe my journey was my gift.

A MOTHER'S POINT OF VIEW

These notes are from my dear mother. I hope they share light with any parents dealing with any eating disorder.

> My intention for you, the reader, is to show how I dealt with what was happening to my daughter. I started to notice physical changes when she was sixteen years old.
>
> I didn't register that things were going on until we were at Tuncurry Golf Club and Amanda, one of Meg's friends, came out and said Meg's been sick in the bathroom. That same day we were in a shopping centre and the three of us weighed ourselves and Meg's reaction surprised me when she realised she was the heaviest out of the three.
>
> I realised something was not right, but started

to hide it as I was concerned about my partner's reaction. As Meg became emaciated, it was obvious that things were going wrong quite quickly.

She wanted to drop some subjects, she was still swimming, her collar was hanging off her and she was still competing in many sports—always on the go.

I was timekeeping at an athletics event. I didn't expect what I saw next because she always won … The wrong person crossed the line.

Meg came last. I had expected her to win.

I finally acknowledged that I was in deep shit and so was she.

She admitted to a friend that something was going on, but I still found it difficult to talk to others about it for fear of what they may think.

I was devastated. I felt I had failed her. Guilt was constantly on my mind and it plagued my thoughts and behaviours every day.

My dialogue was along the lines of *I think I could have done things better, from my perspective.* My upbringing influenced how I thought and I kept thinking on the should haves, could haves and would haves. This was exhausting.

The could haves are irrelevant.

I *could have* done things differently ...

I *could have* been more open ...

I tried to hide it and *could have* done things with more awareness ...

I blamed myself.

I struggled with the fact that her maths and English went down. I tried to constantly be the 'fixer' and make it better, but nothing seemed to work. In fact, it probably pushed her further away.

These words never should be told.

'Once you have an eating disorder, you will always have an eating disorder,' the nutritionist said.

Meg was nineteen when she was told this and there followed a considerable shift from anorexia to bulimia because no tools were provided, just re-feeding, meal plans and processed food. Nothing was taught. Nothing was learnt.

Suicide was on my ever-blaring radar and I witnessed through her journals that this had been considered. I was scared and withdrawn, and still felt the need to hide it and pretend we were going to be OK. Even though I knew I wanted to soften, to say it's not OK, I couldn't help trying to pretend that it wasn't as bad as it was.

I thought it was all my fault. This played in my brain for more than twenty-five years.

I now realise that it was going to happen anyway. There was no way in the world I could change it. Meg chose to do it her way and nothing was going to change that. And she finally found her way out. No one can 'fix' you. It has to be done from the inside out.

I can look back now and see that nothing I did changed the way that Megs had her ride. As a mother, I encourage you to put the energy back into yourself and show compassion and love when you feel fear and know that you are doing the best you can. None of what other people go through, even your kids, is ever your fault.

I believe this guilt that I held on to for so long presented itself in my body, and I am slowly starting to get to know the connection between my thoughts and my physiological response.

If I leave a message or word of advice for any mothers, fathers or carers for kids with an eating disorder, it is that I would have chosen at the start to realise it was not my fault. And the best thing is to be there whenever needed. I would have not tried to fix it or hide from it, but show my own vulnerability and acceptance that I was suffering too. It's not about not supporting them; it's about being there, stepping back and allowing with compassion. It is not about taking the blame for the choice they made.

It's only when you realise what you are thinking—the blame, shame and guilt—that you are able to do something about it and make a choice to support them, but not hold on to a belief that this is your fault.

Otherwise, you will struggle with this for years, wishing and hoping for a different outcome that was completely out of your control.

You're fighting against something you can't defeat or change. Surrender how you think it should be, let go of the wheel, put the energy back into yourself, your health, your self-care, and just be there. The journey for them will unfold and all they need is your love.

Get help for your family and friends who are going through it, reach out to others, get to understand the second person that is Ana (anorexia) or Mia (bulimia). Understand what information is out there that is being digested by your loved one and have a clear view of current trends and groups that may be encouraging this behaviour.

It's important to understand that your child and

your child's eating disorder are two very separate things. When nasty, condescending, hurtful and painful words come out of their mouths, you have a choice to not take it on board and not make it personal.

It is not worth holding on to the thought that you caused something that your child has made a choice to practice. Offer yourself compassion and kindness, and show up the best you can for yourself. This is the best bit of information and support that you can offer your child when they are travelling through this time.

Don't hesitate to lean on someone. Not much was available to me at the time when we went through this, and I felt terrified, unsupported, and fearful that she was going to die. Megs has shared with me three support systems that are amazing not only for people suffering an eating disorder, but for parents and carers as well.

- Millie Thomas—an eating disorder survivor and recovery coach (@millietnz on Instagram)
- Beyond Blue—beyondblue.org.au
- endED—a holistic facility on Queensland's Sunshine Coast

With love x
Robyn

YOU'RE NOT PRETTY ENOUGH TO BE ON OUR TEAM

I took someone else's words and made them my story.

The words in this story's title were the underlying belief I held for twenty-eight years of my life—from age six to age thirty-four.

And I am so grateful, as this was meant to be my ride so that I can now be here.

My anorexia decided to show her face at the tender age of fifteen years. For many years, we all thought, including me, that it had *just happened*. Someone said something about my thighs or weight on a scale. But from my studies, I now understand our beliefs, our thoughts, the words we speak, and the experiences that we cling to or resist, shape our future patterns and actions. This is where we dive into *Watch YA Language*.

This is not a story about eating disorders. That will be another book. This is a story about how we, as humans, can be a whole lot *kinder* to ourselves through the words we speak and the thoughts we think.

We Are Born Bright

The last one to be picked for a game of tunnel ball. I remember standing on my own with my head down, wondering what was wrong with me.

I was six years old. Up until this moment I had been a bouncy, confident, vibrant, energetic and playful kid. I had white-blonde hair, I loved to move (nothing has changed) and I used to dream of playing with horses and unicorns. I would set up secret cubby houses under the kitchen table and on the electric-blue suede lounge we had (yes it was a cracker) and run my imaginary empire from them.

You may notice many young kids have the same vibrant, loud, and assertive energy that is always demanding attention; they are never afraid to speak up or speak their truth, and love to show off in front of you. They are bright and playful, happy to just be themselves and shine.

Of course, this is not the situation with all kids. It depends on how we entered the world and how we were nurtured. But this was most definitely my case.

I believed I was amazing. I had no prior patterns or thoughts that determined otherwise. Up until then.

As I stood there, feeling something I had never felt before—shame—my body was closed, scared, trembling and vulnerable. I had not experienced this before and did not know what to do.

What is wrong with me?

Why am I still standing here?

Why doesn't she like me?

What will everyone think?

Then, out of nowhere, I heard her start to speak. I tilted my head up in a desperate plea and heard the words: 'You're not pretty enough to be on our team. You'll have to go with the other team.'

I barely heard the last words. That statement stung like a bee and sent a dagger deep down in my heart, creating a scar that would last the next twenty-eight years.

And here is where we begin.

The start of limiting beliefs and shitty self-talk

These impressions are known in Eastern religions as *samskaras*, something we either suppress or cling to. If you think back on your own life, you may remember a time when someone mentioned something about you.

A family member, friend or schoolmate might have said you were ...

stupid	fat	boring	ugly
weird	loud	annoying	not worthy

Is it possible that we took those words and created an *I am* ...?

How did this make you feel? I bet you remember it quite well. I invite you to take a moment and sit with this.

Maybe you had a lot of this growing up, and as you started to get older, you took this belief with you and started to dim your light.

You would feel judged if you spoke up about something, and choose to lie or keep quiet instead, believing people would like you better this way.

You started to lose belief in yourself as a person and didn't think you were worthy of doing well, achieving or looking after yourself ... asking the question *Why am I here?*

You may have started to be a chameleon—people pleasing and changing your state for everyone. Trying to be liked by the popular crowd, or to please parents, teachers and others and meet their expectations of you.

Sit with it. What does it feel like to sit with these thoughts? Take a moment to write this down without judgement.

This story of not feeling enough was the driver for my constant perfectionism, my desire to always be right, my burden to be the best, and my determination to please people and feel validated and accepted. All of which are not bad things. But when not recognised, and in excess, are dangerous and addictive.

My dialogue had become a dangerous replay of 'shitty self-talk' that went round and round for years.

What is practised and repeated in our thoughts, words and actions becomes our reality.

So, with much repetition, from the age of six to an impressionable teen, they started to become my way of being. I was a self-obsessed awkward female trying to fit in, doing what I could with the information that I knew to try to survive.

My eating disorder was my choice

That may not sit well with some, but as mentioned, this book is about honesty and integrity and I most definitely had a choice in my reactions to the emotions I didn't want to feel. I just didn't have any other tools.

I will be using that word often. *Choice*. If this book could come down to one word, this would be it.

My hope is that by spending time with your thoughts and the teachings in this book, you will gain the ability to *choose* a kinder way with your words and your reactions, and offer yourself compassion over criticism.

I took the words 'You're not pretty enough' from someone

else, at the age of six, and created the story that was my program for the next twenty-eight years.

If you take anything from this book, I encourage you to *do the work*. Bandaid solutions will get you nowhere. Numbing or running from the things that are difficult will only lead to a life of being controlled by things that took place many years ago that you have not let go. It is important now more than ever to dive deep and start to unravel the uncomfortable layers that have blocked your authenticity and your true self.

Your highest self is dying for you to let them in. You just have to listen, lean in, trust and allow.

The practice of people-pleasing

The Cambridge Dictionary describes a people pleaser as 'someone who cares a lot about whether other people like them, and always wants others to approve of their actions'.

Just reading that sentence makes me feel tired. Using our energy to gain other people's approval takes so much effort.

More, more, more.

At age fifteen I was a very competitive professional swimmer on the brink of Commonwealth Games selection for breaststroke. I was good at what I did, which was no surprise due to the effort, perfection and time I put into the sport.

I was in the era of swimming sensations Liesel Jones and Ian Thorpe, and triathlete Nicole Hackett.

In about 1998 I remember being at Padstow Swim Club for an event, awkward as anything, standing in line (as you do with swim cap on and goggles tucked into cossies) next to a guy that had the biggest feet I had ever seen.

From his feet I looked upwards to meet the gaze of another awkward human, Ian Thorpe.

I vaguely remember an equally awkward conversation, as was the case at swim meets back in those days, about how fast your fifty-metre free was, where you're from (he didn't look very human) and a gentle understanding of … *I'm a little nervous … how 'bout you?*

Swimming was a tough sport then and I believe it's still the same. You are constantly looking for a better time, aiming to be faster than your last meet, and of course, inwardly striving to (unconsciously or not) maintain a fit and toned body because it is always on display. I was also on the constant search for gratification from parents, coaches and others for affirmation of 'how good I was' or that I was 'getting close to the top times'.

I was in the swimming game from about the age of a tadpole, and the conditioning of how I looked slowly started to add to my own insecurities, which had been growing from that previous 'not pretty enough' stab to the heart at the tender age of six.

I don't remember too much from the swimming years, however one thing that did stick with me, and my mum recalls this too, was a comment from another swimmer in line about my thighs being bigger than hers. (Nothing to do with me, though I took it personally at the time.)

Ouch. That drove the dagger a little deeper into my heart. A reminder again of the pain I had experienced, stored and run away from, and that maybe something was wrong with me and my imperfections were something I needed to fix.

I need to fix me

Time for a pause? Do you have the feeling that you need to 'fix you'? Might be an opportunity to start writing again.

Nearly all comments that are judgemental or made with the intention of bullying come from a place of pain and another individual who is also suffering. Can you see how these samskaras (impressions) start to create a block in our bodies and minds?

Over time, from the age of six, I started to make everything personal. I really started to worry what others thought of me. I became a perfectionist. We are not born a perfectionist and it is not, I believe, a personality trait. It's a learnt habit of not feeling enough in who we are, so we strive consistently for perfection and approval.

When practised enough, this starts to become our life and at a young age we move further away from our authentic, unique and beautiful selves.

These days we have the addition of expectations from social media. Apps for body modifications such as Facetune, Meitu and Snow show images of males and females who have altered their skin, waist, thighs, bum, tummy, and everything else you can imagine. Unless you were comparing their image to their original, you would not necessarily know the difference. This scares me and is the backbone of this book.

I have edited my own images on Instagram (@watch. ya.language) to show how easy it is to create a small and almost unnoticeable change that unfortunately is highly addictive and dangerous. More on this later.

Fast forward to my age group … the legendary 'fiery forties'. Well, I'm still thirty-nine at the time of writing this paragraph, but hanging to turn. We have been faced with magazines, billboards, TV, social media, advertising, calorie and fad diets, slimming tea, gym junkies, *Aerobics Oz Style*, G-strings and tiny waists. Very early on, I clearly remember my mother using cling wrap around her waist. It made you sweat more to give you a smaller and more toned figure. I bet she was not the only one who tried that trend back in the day.

These images and experiences create samskaras. If we don't let them move through us we start to subconsciously create a belief that we need to look a certain way to be successful, popular and liked.

Why are we so stuck on judging and comparing ourselves to others? Why are we not happy with what we have been gifted? And the awkward but very real question: why do we sabotage ourselves the way we do? Eating too much, eating too little. Worrying about how we look, our hair, photos, what others will think of us if we do or say X. Hating what we see in the mirror, modifying our bodies to look like our Snapchat filters (yes that's a 'thing' and we will be diving into it) ... wishing we were somewhere else, doing something else, feeling energised, doing what we love with a someone who makes us happy, earning a certain amount of money, nailing the 'perfect' job ... looking like the cool kids, with the perfect body ...

My friend, it's time you realised something. If you are always looking, you'll always be searching. Instead of constantly being on the hunt for more, learn to appreciate what you already have. You are enough without the need for more.

Baseline Message

I got stuck on some words someone said and I chose to believe them. Think about that for a second. For more than twenty-eight years I chose to believe this story that was not even mine. This is crazy. And I hope you can see how we can easily turn a thought into our reality through years and years of giving power to that story.

This was my journey, and I will always be doing the work. This hopefully can be a book that delivers questions we are forced to face, not with judgement or criticism, but with curiosity and compassion.

My story hopefully can spark this question for you: *Is there a story that I have not been able to heal? Was there pain or suffering that I haven't really addressed yet that I still judge myself on or label myself with?*

Every time we investigate and dive into our layers, our dark secrets and our trauma, it's important to do so with a compassionate and open heart. You will learn through this book that opening your heart is key for letting go of the things that we are holding on to. It will take time, and forgiveness, and it's quite likely to be painful, raw and real.

But absolutely nothing in my life or yours is worth hanging onto. Blaming, shaming, or holding on to guilt will only occur later in life.

So here is to *you* and starting to find more space and authenticity, and moving towards your highest self by choosing to be kinder to yourself, through your thoughts and with your words.

Journal moment

What can you find in these teachings that resonates with an experience from your childhood? Were there some big things that went deep into your heart? These experiences are the key to unravelling your blocks. We will explore this over the course of this book.

Affirmation

I am now here. I completely accept and acknowledge all my choices up until this moment. I am ready to create change. I choose to learn to love the skin I'm in.

The practice

From RIGHT NOW I want you to commit to twenty-minute practice of starting to put YOU FIRST. I want you to start to lean in.

Please visit my YouTube channel, Meg Linton, and search for 'The Practice'. Simplicity is key, and overcomplication is not what we need. A more detailed description and examples are in the five-minute video.

Your day will look like this ...

- Ten minutes in the morning
- Ten minutes at night

If you are already thinking *I don't have the time*, then you need to do twenty minutes in the morning and twenty minutes at night.

AM

1. First thing upon waking, say 'Thank you.' You get to have today. Then, set a snooze button for five minutes, place your hand on your heart, and repeat in your mind your affirmations (find some on watchyalanguage.com under Resources). They are to be said with emotion. You need to create energy behind them.

2. Do not check your phone.

   Go to your safe space at home and write down your affirmations in a book, notepad or diary. Read them again and feel them like they are already happening. Look at yourself in the mirror and say, 'You are amazing. I choose to be kind to you today,' and smile. Choose to *accept* what you see and get right behind it.

   Go about your day and practise being curious, not critical; responsive, not reactive.

3. Read your vision statement (there is a template in the back of this book for you to fill out), and yes, stack all those feel-good emotions behind it.

PM

1. Before bed, take between ten and thirty minutes to ease into your night routine. Get off your phone, do some yin yoga (there are more than one hundred and fifty practices on my YouTube), and write down three things you are grateful for.

2. Spend ten minutes in absolute silence. Let it be what it is; just keep practising. Things will come up. Be the observer and watch them without clinging or making a story out of them. Remember, this is a practice.

Repeat every day for the rest of your life.

I guarantee you have twenty minutes spare. Just track how much time you spend on your device.

The way you feel about yourself and your worthiness is completely in your hands. These are the tools. Do them just like you hop in the shower, do your teeth and jump on your Instagram feed. You are entirely up to you.

LOSING THE AUTHENTIC SPARK–DIMMING THE LIGHT

Bronnie Ware, in her book *The Top Five Regrets of the Dying*, says:

> When we are born we are like light globes. We bounce around, we are confident, we speak our truth and shine bright. Over the years we start to get stuff thrown at our light globe, and we throw stuff back at others.
>
> As the stuff hits our globe, the light is still shining however it gets a little murky inside. We start to dim our lights and not shine so bright or cheerful, we start to become the darkness rather than the light and we forget who we are as the external is now covered in layers, dirt, messiness and pain.

The number-one regret is I wish I had had the courage to live a life true to myself, not the life others expected of me.

Hopefully by gaining an understanding from this book of your patterns and addictions, you can start to apply what you learn to a new way of being so that you get to the end of your life feeling fulfilled, content and happy with what you have, with no regrets, no holding on, no guilt and no shame. It was perfect, just how it unfolded.

This teaching is something that really resonated with me as I watched my dear nan really battle with the last three years of her life.

Surrender yourself fully and give yourself permission to let it go, for nothing in this life is worth keeping in your heart, brain and body.

My biggest teacher

She was a determined, stubborn, beautiful by-the-book lady who would do anything for her family. She always put others first and made sure she made a fuss over you whenever she could. She had white, slightly crazy grandma hair, and wore pink cardigans that smelt of tea and Anzac cookies. She sat in the same patterned cream chair and offered fruit cake (that I always pretended to love) every time we visited.

She was bold yet soft, and had a true heart of gold, especially for her girls. She stood by her beliefs and there was no way you could change her mind when she was onto something.

She was old-school.

She was a rock.

And she was full of love, but she was always putting others first.

Nan was the most incredible teacher I could have asked

for. She taught me kindness, compassion, drive, and above all, surrender.

As mentioned, this book was not ready until my nan passed. We will uncover why in the last story, and hopefully I can share this message, filled with so much gratitude, with you.

She was born in the 1920s and lived to an amazing ninety-seven years young.

Those last few years, however—from what *I* observed—were torture for her. Inner pain, emotions and frustrations started to surface and she became a shadow of the woman she was. She just wanted to go, but the deep pain and trauma from her past that had not been felt or expressed started to come to the surface and present. As a family we all witnessed a darker change in her behaviour, words and actions.

Whatever had happened in her past was an event that she shared with only a few of us. The event is irrelevant. The situation, however, caused a block of seventy years of unspoken and unforgiven heartache, pain and shame.

Back then, she was told it was never to be spoken about. It had to be bottled up and never visited again. That was often the case, not just for my nan, but for many other families in that generation. Do you remember the saying 'girls are seen and not heard' or 'big girls don't cry' or maybe 'put a smile on that dial'?

Generations ago, bottling things up was a very well-practised habit. (Maybe you can also relate to this with your own family.) When you are in your nineties, however, the energy has nowhere to go but out if you do not allow yourself to feel it. There were moments where she would write *Help me* on the walls of the hospital, scream in the nursing home, and believe we were being taken over by the Russians. There were other moments that were not her, but it seemed her thoughts and fears had become her. The words she spoke of herself were judgemental and hurtful;

she spoke of being 'a horrible person' and 'unable to forgive herself'.

These last two phrases were voiced on her last day in the nursing home whilst she struggled with the fear of death at her doorstep, the suffering of past events not healed, and an almighty physical resistance to receiving love.

This dialogue does not just start in your nineties or in your last years ... for Nan, it had been practised for years. The way I see it, that is absolutely not a way for any of us to live.

I share this from the deepest intention of love, for the opportunity to maybe spark a thought in you to lean in and do the work on your self. It is ridiculously painful, and I honour you for even reading this far, but it is more painful to live a life bound by our regrets, past experiences, shame, anger and guilt. How are we able to help others and give back when we are burdened by an old story and belief of our past?

My hope is that this book will support you to gently, and without judgement, open the blinkers just enough to allow you to think about sparking your own healing journey, the one that is available to you right now, in this moment. This is an opportunity to be guided forward now with love, compassion and—above all—acceptance that it all has unfolded perfectly right up to this moment.

You made it, right? You are here reading these pages. Look at how far you have come and imagine what abundance, love and acceptance lies ahead for you after finishing this book and embracing the practices. You've got this and I see you.

Nan, you have delivered to me the biggest gift that I could ever receive. The ability to acknowledge with compassion the messiness of my past and trauma (we all have some!), to give myself permission to feel the emotions that I may have pushed down, and to forgive—when the time is right (God will show me)—the trauma, pain and suffering that is no longer part of my current story.

We are not born angry, frustrated, and unforgiving of ourselves. We are open, we shine bright, and we are at peace with ourselves. Something has to have been stored within for us to react like this. A belief, a past event, trauma, a regret ... a samskara.

This is where our light globe is so fogged over that we forget who we are, and we live in a world of our shame, guilt and blame.

It is up to us to choose to not let our past occupy our future.

Let's learn to understand how we can start to undo these layers.

So what the hell is a samskara?

When I got my head around samskaras and understood what they were and how many I had packed like sardines in my body since I was a little girl, I started to get it. I was like, whoa ... I'm glad I am learning about this now, so that I can do something about them and try to create some space in my mind and my body.

So I'll do my best to share the very basics over the next story or two, in the hope that you can pass this information on to your kids as well to help them understand that *nothing* is worth holding on to. Nothing.

Your heart will be the driver of your thoughts. If we do not feel love, compassion or acceptance for ourselves, our mind will be filled with the wish to be enough, accepted and validated.

I speak with students about this when I work in high schools. I get them to answer a question: When we feel jealousy, love or pain, where is it felt?

It's felt in the heart, right? Not in the head.

Our thoughts are felt in our head. They are visual and verbal. They can create images that are extremely solid and real. In essence, when we give attention to a thought, we can create a full story.

And funnily enough, that story comes true if we keep paying attention to it, right?

A deeper dive on the heart

The thoughts we experience are generated from the vibration that is pulsing out of our heart. E-motion (energy in motion).

If we are feeling love, gratitude or acceptance, our thoughts will match that vibe, our bodies will be open and receptive, and our mind calm. We are present.

The opposite is also true if we are feeling shame, guilt, blame, worry or fear. The vibration that comes from that feeling emanates up out of the heart space to our thoughts and we judge, self-sabotage and become wrapped up in the story that our thoughts are creating.

The heart, I believe, is a true teacher. It's something I could talk about for hours, but I'll save that for my next book. My intention is to have you *curious*, not *critical* about what you are feeling and experiencing on a daily basis.

It's perfectly normal if you have just completely freaked out. *I don't want to feel my heart,* you may be thinking. *I've been running from and numbing those emotions and feelings all my life.*

If you don't start to show up for them, then they are going to run you, my friend. And you'll take the things that you have clung to or suppressed with you until your last day. Is that really a way to live life?

Your choice. Again, you are here to dive in with compassion and curiosity.

These words are delivered here not to judge, but to invite gentle self-inquiry. Trust the process and know that you are here for a reason. This is not a book to be rushed; it's a book to help you soften to the possibility that there is something under the pain, the illness, the patterns, the addictions and the dialogue. Be kind to yourself and take your time.

Get to understand what keeps us stuck

Take a moment to separate the heart and the mind. In the heart we *feel*; in the mind we *see*.

The mind is an amazing tool and is really fascinating when we can sit back and watch it. We may understand, however, that if we hang out in our heads too long, our thoughts start to become our reality.

Good or not so good. Energy flows where attention goes. Which garden are you wishing to water? This choice is on us.

How we start to shift our self-talk is what many call 'doing the work'.

If we have been watering the garden of beliefs that contain the stories of not feeling enough, unworthiness and little self-love ... then that garden will be abundant with more of the same.

Start to practise watering the other garden, and, well ... this is what you will see grow.

So choose wisely where you put your attention, and with the BE HERE method that I share in this book, I hope that by the end of these pages you will start to simply notice the voice inside your head and witness it without judging it.

It's always talking to you. It's our job, though, to become the watcher of our thoughts, understand they are not us and with awareness interrupt the (familiar) neurological pathways, and choose again.

Note that we are *always* feeling something. You are the one inside that is *experiencing* the feeling or the thought. But it's not you.

You are also the one who is seeing your body, but it is not you.

Digest this for a second. When *you* judge your own body, it's the voice inside your head telling you, *I wish I could be ten kilos lighter. Why can't my tummy look like hers? I hate my thighs ... if only they were smaller.* And you hear back something like, *Get to the gym you fatty ... go and burn off the ice-cream you ate last night so you can fit into those jeans.* And so on.

As someone who went through many eating disorders for nearly thirty years, I can attest that the voice inside your head is constantly on replay, reminding you of the limiting beliefs, stories and judgements that you hold on yourself. But I had no idea at the time that I could choose to be the witness of the thoughts and step away from them. To understand that the thoughts were not me and that I had a choice.

This is a conversation going on inside of you.

You are not the one talking: the mind is. You are experiencing it. You are hearing the conversation and noticing it going on.

So, if you are noticing the conversation, it's *not you*.

You are the one who *sees*.

This is the first step of the BE HERE method I'll discuss a little later.

When you understand this, it is huge. You realise you are the soul, the watcher, the observer, the one who is aware that you are *experiencing* everything that lands in front of you (moments). But it is up to you if you choose to hold on to the moment, make a story out of it, or suppress it deep in your heart where you think it has been forgotten.

This is what 'being triggered' is really about

Picture this.

You come home from work after a big day and realise you are still fuming over what your manager said to you at a meeting: 'I'm not sure it hits the mark. Maybe see if you can express the message in another way.'

What the voice inside your head might have thought is this. *She's judging me and thinks it's terrible. I'm so shit. I always have been since [insert name] said so back in [insert year]. What did I expect when I presented that? What's the point anyway? Whatever I come back with will be shot down. I may as well just leave and they can find someone better than me.*

It's highly likely your manager did not think that about you at all. She merely wanted you to try another idea that fitted her image of what was needed. But you decided to believe a story.

Based on what? A moment you held on to?

Why? Because it triggered your shit.

It triggered something familiar that you experienced many years ago when you didn't get into an art exhibition and felt excluded and not enough.

You held on to this moment, and by holding on and suppressing it, you created an impression, a samskara, a blockage in your energy flow.

So whenever someone or something presses this button, the heart is triggered. Energy (emotion) vibrates from your heart upwards and you feel a change. Your mood has gone from playful and fun to judgemental and critical.

In that moment at work (and then for hours after) you feel small, unheard, unworthy, stupid and whatever other emotions may be bubbling up.

Your body starts to tense and you have a splitting headache. You have overeaten due to stress and worry and are feeling anxious to replay the situation to your partner who also said something the other month that resonates with this story. You think about calling by the local bottle shop to get a bottle of wine to numb out the evening. Maybe they were right. You are stupid after all.

I'm repeating this. It is *so important* to understand that the only reason we are triggered is because of the things we are holding on to. Remember back at the start, I said this: I took someone else's words and turned them into *my* story.

There has been something, someone, a job, a car, a house, an achievement or a body in your past where you have created what is called an 'attachment'.

This has been an experience that you didn't like and it didn't make you feel good. Or it was the opposite: it was so good, you compare everything to that moment.

So you pushed it down deep, or clung to it in your heart, and ignored the feelings that were meant to be felt way back in that moment many years ago. You held on. And possibly still do.

If we are in a situation where we are being triggered, this means there is something we have clung to or resisted, and the environment we are in is reminding us of the same experience five, ten or twenty years ago. We haven't actually allowed ourselves to clear the blockage, the samskara.

The *only* reason we are triggered is because there is something inside of us that we have not healed yet … that's all.

Breathe out, place your hand on your heart and take a moment of compassion. It's OK. We *all* have these samskaras. Now you are going to learn how to offer them compassion, acknowledge them for what they are and give yourself permission to forgive, feel them and heal them. I can't help but share the words of one of my beautiful friends, Morag Joseph, here: 'We learn to mindfully unfuck ourselves.'

Your body will tell you

It's not about judging the samskara. This is what this book is about. It's about being curious as to why we have held on, and from this moment, what are we going to do about it. Do we choose to start to let go, or continue to feed the fire that does not serve us.

So, if the feeling and emotion is in the heart, and it's one of judgement, criticism or shame, what then happens to the physical body?

It tenses, closes, contracts. It becomes a body and mind that doesn't let anything in. Think of an animal or small child when they are trying to protect themselves—there is tension, reactivity, and activation of the sympathetic nervous system. We will discuss this later.

This tensing and closing is the body reacting to the ripple effect of an emotion. It's a vibration. Some ripple effects are larger than others—the bigger the emotion, the bigger the experience. It's a way to protect ourselves from getting hurt, so we run from the heart up to the mind. This is where we create a story to hide from what it is we are unwilling to feel.

On the flipside is the body's response to love, compassion and kindness felt in the heart space. These emotions (vibrations) will emanate from your heart space into your aura, what people see and feel. Your body will be open, your face kind; you will seem approachable and calm.

This also *feels* so much better and we take a load off, choose our stresses, and learn slowly to surrender more and let go.

We are also going to dive into the very basics of neuroplasticity, which hopefully will give you the tools to get to know your brain and an understanding of when you are reactive rather than responsive.

In closing (for now) on the exciting topic of the heart, if we have experienced a low feeling or emotion on a constant basis— say for example, someone such as a carer, teacher, parent or relative telling us we were never going to achieve our dreams as we were not smart enough like the rest of the kids—we might start to believe this story. We can then hear a repeat of this story through school, college, work and so on. (Similar to what I described earlier.)

We can also experience shame and guilt in our heart at a young age if we have done something (which is what kids do) and someone has told us how bad we have been, how embarrassed they are because of the choice we made, or how shamed they feel due to our actions or behaviours. This could be a reflection of possible unhealed shame or guilt in the person who tells us how wrong we have been, and there is the possibility that this has been passed down through generations.

So, from a very young age, we try to modify ourselves to make others happy and to make sure we keep the peace, not speak up, be a good child and be on our 'best' behaviour. Sometimes, we can miss out on being kids altogether.

We start to believe that being ourselves is not what the world is looking for or likes, so we try to fit in, we put on our masks, and we try to be what the external expects of us. We then ride the constant hamster wheel of perfection and pleasing people for as long as we choose. Sound familiar?

We start to contract and close and become small, as that's what we believe we are. That is our interpretation.

The thoughts are repetitive and consistent. And then we start to hear other things that people say, and we start to believe it to be true.

It's repeated often in this book, but what we practise is what will grow.

Research shows we have between sixty thousand and seventy thousand thoughts per day, and more than ninety per cent of those are the same. Most of us are living in our programmed mind, which generates from the last trimester of birth (yes, we take on our mother's energy when they are pregnant) to about the age of reason: seven.

This is our paradigm. This is our blueprint of limiting beliefs for the rest of our life, if we don't stop to become aware.

And awareness is where it's all at.

So, going back to the connection between the heart, body and thought, if it's a shitty feeling in your heart—shame, blame, guilt, fear, jealousy, anger, frustration, doubt, helplessness or judgement—our words will reflect that feeling, and our physical state will reflect that energy.

The self-talk that you speak ripples from your thoughts, which vibrate from a feeling in your heart.

So, let's begin the process of working on changing the *feeling* in our heart to shift our energy ... our vibration.

> ### Journal moment
> I want you to write this below in your journal.
> When I feel [insert emotion] my body does [insert reaction].

You will notice the body has a somatic (physical) reaction when you feel an emotion. Emotion relates to the body especially, as distinct from the mind.

If you find you are on the lower part of the scale, do your best to acknowledge the emotion and see what you can do for yourself to slowly move up the scale. This is great to practice with kids too.

For example, say your child is feeling discouraged from an incident that happened in the schoolyard. You could have a chat about what happened and how they feel, and ask what would make them feel better. I imagine slowly they will start to light up as they think of what they love or are passionate about. If it's soccer, or playing with the dog, take five or ten minutes to go and do that and see their heart light up as they move up the scale past boredom and then possibly to hopefulness.

We can do the same as adults. Notice the emotion, acknowledge it and come back to asking, *What does my heart need right now?* (We'll cover this later in Step 3 of the BE HERE method.)

Scale of emotions from 1–22

1. Joy, appreciation, empowerment, freedom, love
2. Passion
3. Enthusiasm, eagerness, happiness
4. Positive expectation, belief
5. Optimism
6. Hopefulness
7. Contentment
8. Boredom
9. Pessimism
10. Frustration, irritation, impatience
11. Overwhelm
12. Disappointment
13. Doubt
14. Worry
15. Blame
16. Discouragement
17. Anger
18. Revenge
19. Hatred, rage
20. Jealousy
21. Insecurity, guilt, unworthiness, shame
22. Fear, grief, desperation, despair, powerlessness

We have a somatic response in our bodies when we feel something.

Now let's go a little deeper.

Where does your mind go?

Next, write down:

My mind experiences [insert your thoughts].
Hopefully you can see that the body, spirit (heart) and mind are all connected.

Mine used to go something like this:

When I feel shame, my body is rigid and tense. My shoulders round in, my heart closes and I am reactive, not responsive.

In my heart I feel NOT ENOUGH, UNWORTHY and SMALL.

In my mind I am thinking, *You need to do better, you're stupid, no one will like you, you don't deserve anyone's love, you need to be smarter and prettier to be liked … you're never going to be enough.*

This language practised daily got me nowhere fast. The only way to change it is to be aware of the story we are creating.

And of course, I repeated the same thoughts, words and behaviours. When we constantly practise thoughts of inadequacy, we start to believe they are true. And, if we don't catch these thoughts and change them, nearly ninety per cent of them will be the same day after day. You've been there, right? Me too.

And that's where the downhill spiral of our thoughts can start and get out of control if we don't learn how to watch our language.

I promise you right now though, if I can be where I am today in my body and mind, with the ability to ground myself with an acceptance and contentment I never thought possible, I guarantee you can too.

Empower yourself and be the practitioner.

You are always a teacher and a student

There are many others who talk about the mind, thoughts and our brain. Rather than dive in more here, I would love to recommend a few teachings from those who have helped me understand my brain.

The ones who stand out to me are Dr Joe Dispenza, Dr Daniel Siegel (*Mindsight*), Bessel van der Kolk (*The Body Keeps the Score*), and locally, and a great friend, Mel Carbis-Reilly (*Diggin' Your Dark Side* and *Becoming*).

These authors go into great detail about the mind, and I have spent nearly seven years researching the brain. Why? Because I needed to change my story, my dialogue, and my language from self-sabotage, doubt and body shaming, and I needed to learn how to accept what I had, appreciate my body exactly as it was, and say thank you for each day that was gifted to me.

This took time, and I highly recommend investing time back into you, as these things do not happen fast.

I needed to understand why my patterns kept repeating themselves, kept happening; why things weren't getting better with age, but worse. This became my drive for delving into myself, my mind, my thoughts in an attempt to do my best to change my outcome so that I could move away from my noisy, disruptive, annoying and self-sabotaging thoughts and words.

Whatever patterns, thoughts and words we have practised—

and yes, they have been a practice—will take time to undo.

Give yourself time

Take a moment and ask yourself, *Am I worth it?*

Are you worth the investment? How would it feel to start to be kinder and more accepting of yourself?

Of course you damn well are. We are all here to give back. You would not be reading this book otherwise. You *know* deep down that you are here for a very good reason.

There is an old story of a tribe in Africa that states this: We are each a blessing to the world. Every one of us is here to deliver our cargo. If we go through life carrying our cargo around and not allowing ourselves to share it, serve it back and deliver it, we lead a life of suffering.

Please let me remind you. You are here for a reason.

Keep reminding yourself of this if you are faced with any resistance: resistance is an old limiting belief you have created over the years. I'm sure this old belief is not true for you anymore.

I urge you to ask yourself with curiosity *Is this true for me anymore?* Do I really need to fuel this fire? You are more than worthy. We all are. Your existence, your light and your story need to be heard, shared and expressed.

Like me, you have probably spent way too long suppressing. Holding yourself back for fear of judgement from others, of what they will think of you, of the terrifying experience of people not accepting you for who you are.

You are the only one who needs to accept yourself. Your tribe will find you and grow your light.

What do those around you see?

Let's stay real here. Maybe you have kids? How are their patterns, words and thoughts? Are they similar to yours?

Remember, this book is about being honest. Really honest.

No judgement. Myself included.

Maybe they copy your eating habits. Maybe they use your dialogue when describing how they see themselves.

Possibly, they look in the mirror and judge their bodies. Are they using apps on their phones to modify, smooth and touch up their bodies and faces?

Do they adapt for others and shy away, scared to speak up for fear of not being liked by others?

Know that none of this is judging, but we really need to call out our own actions and habits in order to move forward. Fostering our awareness is the only way we can change.

And when we change, others around us start to notice that we are putting ourselves first and our energy starts to vibrate a little higher, sending what we need back to us.

Trying to fix the world and those around us is like leading a horse to water, and then watching as it refuses to drink.

On a side note, during regular speaking engagements in Newcastle and the NSW north coast, the most commonly asked question is: 'My kids are suffering from [insert condition]. What can I do to fix them? I've tried everything.'

You can never fix another, but you can use that energy and put it back into you.

As mentioned at the start, I do not have the answer. However, from my experience, I believe the best thing we can do if our kids are going through turmoil, self-sabotage, mental health struggles, eating disorders or anxiety is to do our best to *show* not *tell*. As hard as that may sound, if you put that energy back into you and you are able to shine by example, you can be a guide for your little ones. You are always their teacher. As they say: be the light you wish to see in the world.

I reply to that question the best I know how, asking the parent: 'Do you think you are compassionate towards yourself? Do you like what you see when you look in the mirror, or find you are also judging, comparing, or searching for more?'

It usually sparks some deep thought to lean in and do the work.

I have not yet received a punch in the face, but do understand it can be triggering. And I ask you, if this does trigger you, can you use your trigger as your teacher and change the dialogue to represent kindness rather than comparison?

Journal moment

How would your kids respond if you started to back yourself more and believe in your beautiful, real and imperfect self?

Spend as long as you need to feel into this and write down your answer as a letter to yourself.

This is why we need to understand what is keeping us blocked in these old patterns.

The river needs to flow—understanding samskaras

Visualise for a moment a stream. I am writing this book in the gorgeous NSW northern hinterland in the Byron Shire and have spent time at Killen Falls.

I am sitting by the water's edge watching the waterfall cascade down into the swimming hole. The water flows on through some rapids downstream and eventually to the ocean.

It has been windy and a little wild, and there is a fair bit of debris in the water—sticks, twigs, leaves—so the water is messy, bubbly and a little angry.

Our samskaras are the rocks and twigs. They block the flow of our energy through our body. These are the things we have either held on to, or resisted (pushed away) in our lifetime.

Get to know what is keeping us stuck

I hope to share with you one of the most profound teachings I have ever experienced: getting to know how these samskaras affect who we are today.

We have all been conditioned from our past somehow. Whether it be a comment like I mentioned in the first story; what we saw our parents, friends, teachers or carers do in their lives; TV commercials; influencers or magazines. This all has played a huge part in the conditioning or programming of our subconscious mind.

In short, samskaras leave an indent.

Perhaps we really don't enjoy a moment and it's unpleasant, so we push it down and suppress it, which of course stores it in our bodies.

At the other end of the scale, perhaps we hold on to a moment that was incredibly amazing, and we cling to it. We then unconsciously compare many other moments (partners, experiences, jobs, our bodies) to it and we are never satisfied as we are trying to replicate the same experience.

So we have held on one way or another.

These are pieces of your life's experiences, good or bad, that you have chosen to hang on to for one reason or another. They block your energy.

These 'blocks' will keep presenting in your *now* existence because life happens around us. In my case, the belief of the story of 'not enough' resurfaced consistently as I grew up and faced rejection, didn't make sports teams, got C grades in some subjects and got fired from a job.

This all triggered the old story and reaffirmed the limiting belief as I had not let it go.

So, in short, by reacting in these situations and judging myself—thinking I was unworthy and blaming others around me—I wasn't living in the present so I couldn't that it had nothing to do with me. I was living right back in the past, experiencing the wound of the little girl aged six.

The same goes with the things we cling to.

Using a body for example, if we are always trying to get back to the body that we had five or ten years ago, we are missing out on what is here now. We need to appreciate what we have and accept it as it is, as it is from this space only that we are able to work towards the person we are becoming from a place of love and compassion.

So, when we are triggered, I believe it is a good thing.

We need to use our triggers as our teachers, and get curious about *why* we are experiencing this reactivity. Use your reactivity to say *Thank you, I understand there is something here that I need to work through,* and (lucky you now have a book in your hands and a method to help you with this) then it is up to you to do the work and unravel the old story.

At the end of the day, absolutely *nothing* is worth holding on to. Like waves of the ocean, moments should pass through us. It is our *choice* as to how long we hold on to them.

Otherwise, we will spend our whole life being defined by our past, which, in my eyes, is not a way any of us deserve to live in the present moment.

I hope you agree and feel an urgency to *let the stuff go.*

When the shit hits the fan

Society conditions us to numb ourselves or run as soon as the shit hits the fan. I believe we all understand with our intuition that whatever we have experienced, we need to feel to heal.

So, in my own story, when I heard the words 'you're not pretty enough', what do you think happened here?

I was six. I had never experienced this feeling before and believed I was a confident, beautiful, fun and playful kid. This made me think otherwise, but most of all, as I mentioned before, it cut like a knife. Right to the heart space. Ouch.

At six, I didn't know what to do so I buried it and tried not to feel it. I didn't talk about it as not too much was talked about in my family. This was just the way it was. We only know what we know. We're a soldier-on, buckle-up buttercup kinda crew, so I got used to holding things in and pushing them down.

This carried on for many years: choosing with my willpower to hold down and suppress the emotions I didn't want to feel.

I bottled it up, buried it deep, forgot about it, put on my big-girl boots and tried to please the fuck out of everyone by being the best at everything I could do. Perfection, pleasing and lying became some of my personal traits at that time to try to be liked, accepted and of course ... enough.

Slowly, I started to lose my sparkle and my authenticity. I felt over the years I became very serious and very competitive, and was on a constant mission to be perfect. I'm so grateful I didn't grow up with the pressures of social media, filter apps such as Facetune, Snow and Meitu, and influencers who seem to portray a 'perfect' body, life and existence.

The world is very different now but the problems and the language remain the same. My hope for you is that by changing your own language and dialogue, you will be able to give permission to the younger generations to do the same. Monkey see, monkey do.

Remember, what we practise grows stronger.

You are always a teacher to someone.

Journal moment

Take time here to express moments in your childhood where you felt the need to impress others, lie to make others happy, or possibly store experiences deep in your heart to not be felt again. Be gentle as you write this down and simply observe what comes up without judging or needing to fix it.

This is what I know

Losing my spark meant slowly moving away from who I was at a soul level. I was slowly replacing my bright, bubbly, messy and playful personality with a sense of low self-worth, addiction to perfection and people pleasing, and living my life for others, not wanting to embrace who I was. I believed no one liked me as I was. So I had to try to be someone else.

Throughout the stories in this book I will keep referencing the samskaras so that hopefully you can gain an understanding of this energy, and how by holding on to experiences, trying to grasp the high moments, or burying and pushing away the awkward and uncomfortable ones, you only create more sticks and twigs in your flow. You start to block your natural flow of vibrant energy and your body has to work harder to maintain its balance.

By doing this, we get knocked out of equilibrium and we begin the debilitating journey of dis-ease, inflammation, exhaustion, and of course, shitty dialogue. By *choosing* to hold on, we keep ourselves stuck in the patterns and beliefs of the past that then present in the current self.

We are bound by our limitations. Without clearing these impressions, we are letting them run, or ruin, our lives. We do our best, all our lives, to avoid being triggered by them.

And if you ask me—and I did this for more than twenty-eight years—this is not a way to live your life. At any moment, we have a choice to choose again, to rewire our brain to believe that we are worthy, we are enough, and we are NOT that old story or limiting belief.

Suppressing emotions, pushing things down to 'not feel' means they will surface again. Maybe you have already experienced this. Maybe not once, maybe it's happened a few times, and yet you shoved it down again.

Maybe one day it will go away.

But energy does not stay still. Not at all.

At six years old I developed a belief that I was not enough. I had a fear that I was unworthy of receiving love and acceptance, and I gave this fear my undivided attention for twenty-eight years. I am a huge believer that our thoughts and dialogue, which stem from the emotions we have stored deep in our subconscious, are the creators of our physical selves.

From lived experience and years of research, I speak with absolute belief that we are able to change our reality when we change the way we think. First, we must acknowledge with compassion where we are at without playing the victim, making excuses, or blaming a situation or event.

This may be challenging to read, so if this triggers you, please take a moment to pause, take a breath and be gentle and open as you read on.

Leaning in to do the work in my mid-thirties, I could feel things were changing. Life got brighter: I witnessed more gratitude, I brought in friends and clients that lifted me up rather than dragging me down, my body started to heal from the gut, I could move better and backbend in my spine, and I started to learn how to handstand and play more, which opened my heart. I started to live.

My movement practice shifted from punishment and pushing in the gym, striving to reach a calorie goal, and the overdoing of fitness classes, to moving to feel good in my body, which triggered a profound physical response. I released tension, my bloating disappeared, and the stress around my organs dissipated; my body became regulated and well. My energy became more vibrant, excited and effortless, and as the years go on since my healing, I am truly pumped about how high I can feel without any stimulus whatsoever.

When we start to clear out the old stories and release the blocks, we really start to experience flow, love and compassion not just for ourselves, but for all human beings.

Being open to teachers such as Michael A. Singer, Dr Daniel Siegel and Dr Joe Dispenza, spiritual teachers such as Louise Hay, Gabby Bernstein and Dr Wayne Dyer, and the study of Ayurveda brought me to the path I am on now. By choosing to change my own thoughts and words through affirmations, self-belief and acceptance, I started to heal my body from the inside out. Recognising with compassion my own emotions of shame, guilt, blame and fear—and the dialogue related to those vibrations—was key to me witnessing the changes in my own body and mind.

This I know to be true: if it can happen for me, I KNOW it can happen for you.

Your authenticity and the choice to do the work is your key to the life you keep dreaming of.

LITTLE MISS PERFECTION

Embrace your imperfections, otherwise you will spend the rest of your life trying to perfect them ... and this task is impossible.

Maybe you're starting to see how these samskaras have shaped our lives up until this moment. It might be a great thing to take some time out when it suits you and do a gentle meditation on acceptance. It is what it is, and you are now here reading these pages.

Whatever brought us to this moment is irrelevant, but what we can do from now is our choice.

Please enjoy this 'Acceptance, Forgiveness and Authenticity' meditation video as a gift with this book: youtube.com/watch?v=hxNN-iXQUpI

Remember, whatever the environment and situation, we always have a choice as to how we respond.

I moved through my life-shaping years (also known as formative years) in a shy, people-pleasing teenage mess. My swimming career started to develop quite strongly—my gymnastics and dancing not so much as I had heavy feet and I was really awkward. Eventually my teachers realised that, with my not-so-co-ordinated body and high energy, ballet was definitely not my thing, which is why I spent many years travelling down the road as a Highland dancer.

(Funny side note here, though. I now get approached quite often to ask if I'm a dancer or gymnast, as I've been told I float or move gracefully. I would never in a million years believe this to be true, but it's a great reminder that we can all change—mind and body.)

Winning was everything to me and losing was not part of my game. I would sulk, I was spoilt, and I got what I wanted. This chapter was going to be called 'The Spoilt Little Brat', as that's what I was.

I was, and still am, a very lucky and blessed daughter. I have been loved fully, and when we understand our love languages, we can appreciate the way we show love to others. This is an important part of my own understanding of my family and the ways that I was brought up. We simply understand that it is what it is; we don't have to agree, and we are not here to be liked by everyone. Hell no. But we are all different and it's so important, especially with family, that respect is given even when beliefs and ways of being are different. We are all human, we are all love at our core, and we are all doing our best. We are all human, we are all born the same and we all are after the same: to find happiness and not suffer.

This way, we can allow great freedom and flexibility to comfort us on a daily basis. Especially right now.

We're all just doing our best

Compassion, responding with kindness rather than reaction, and surrendering the need to be right can be powerful tools to get along better with others when our values and ideas are different.

It's so important to know that we are all just doing our best with the information we know. My mum used to always tell me that she wanted to give me what she didn't have. And I fully respect and honour that, but it did teach me that I could turn it on, cry, carry on and whinge and I could have whatever I wanted. And that I did.

The journey to people pleasing

I learnt that turning on the charm and getting what I wanted created a feeling of happiness for a short while in my brain: a dopamine hit. I would get the toy, the food, the trip out, the clothes, the shoes … and it would feel good for a while, and then I would want more.

This was a dangerous pattern I was starting to cement in my brain. I was forming synaptic connections that would create familiar patterns when I was looking for pleasure, a sense of worth, and happiness. Unfortunately I was looking outside of me to fix a deep sense of 'not enough' that had not healed, and was not going to for a long time.

We have a choice

Reactivity or response? As I mentioned before, in every situation and environment, we have a choice. We have a choice in how we respond, or how we react and take action.

In February 2021, I had the pleasure and humbling experience of meeting Danny Abdallah at one of my talks at Elysia, a NSW wellness retreat.

I was sharing the BE HERE method and spent some time on the difference between response and reactivity.

This man has endured pain and grief like no other.

Danny came up to me after my talk about allowing our feelings to be as they are and to move through them with compassion, love and kindness, and gave me one of the biggest hugs I have ever experienced. I felt all of it. I didn't even know what 'it' was.

He started to talk.

'I choose to forgive.'

I was silent.

'I don't know if you saw it on the news?'

At this point I froze and felt goosebumps rise on my arms.

I don't watch the news, preferring to direct my attention to other things that lift me up, but I knew this was going to be a traumatic twist and spin.

'Go on,' I said.

'I lost my three children Antony, Angelina and Sienna, and my cousin's daughter, Veronique, on 1 February 2020.'

My heart dropped. I went cold.

He continued to talk.

'I had a choice. To either choose to respond or react for myself and my kids. And I choose to respond.'

He showed me a YouTube video of himself speaking at the launch of i4give day, which takes place on 1 February each year. In it he takes about his choice to forgive the drugged-up and drunk driver for what happened that day. The following is a powerful message from Danny on his ability to choose:

I face the choice. The choice that I want you all to comprehend, if there is anything I want to share with you today. What path do I take? The path of destruction, or the path of construction? Do I react and numb this pain, or respond and face

this pain? I choose to respond. I choose to seek my
refuge and my strength. I choose to obey my father
in Heaven and forgive.

What an insanely powerful message.

This man showed courage and strength, and above all
surrendered to what was. He has three other kids to look after
and shine a light for. He chose to show up, respond, not react,
and radiate love and compassion. In the circumstances he faced,
his rare act of selflessness will serve his family with the utmost
offering of acceptance there ever was.

You can check out his page at i4give.com.

'I chose to respond with love, as that is the message I want
my family to see,' Danny said to me. There is a huge difference.

Thank you, Danny. Your teachings and kindness will never
ever be forgotten. You are shining an amazing light out there to
the world.

Our paradigm, the program

I was already struggling with the belief that I was not enough,
so my thoughts were revolving around self-judgement, constant
criticism, low self-worth and a lack of belief. I got better at
affirming this belief by giving it my utmost attention day in, day
out.

In every situation that triggered my samskara—the belief
that I was not pretty enough—I chose to avoid and numb the
feelings and emotions that arose. This numbing and eventually
running from these feelings started an unhealthy practice of
not feeling my feelings, and suppressing them even more in the
hope that they would disappear and fade.

So, in my brain, I was sparking the same connections each
time I was faced with unease, which was often.

Just like branches of a tree, these synaptic connections fire and wire together each time we are faced with a situation. When we react the same way (in my case I would retreat, push down the feelings of unworthiness and shame, and numb or run from them) it just makes the roots stronger for that particular choice.

This cluster of neurons started to become a very large and dense practised pattern.

Dr Daniel says the limbic area is our primal brain: '[It's] the part that drives our emotions. That which motivates us to act in response to whatever is happening to us in that moment.'

Repeated response and action strengthens the neural pathways over time—over many years—so we find we are reacting the same way over and over because we are continually choosing to be in the same environment with our thoughts. Our amygdala, located within the limbic region, gets so used to our constant, stressed 'on' state that it is ready and raring to go at the drop of a hat and keeps us in fight-or-flight mode.

Over years and years of practising numbing my feelings, I created a solid cluster of neurons that were so used to the same reaction that it became familiar to me to choose, as Dr Siegel calls it, 'the low road'. This is the shortest path from our amygdala to our hardwired reactions, which processes fearful and threatening stimuli. When this guy fires, we don't have much time to catch the firing, unless we are present; when we are present, we respond from our prefrontal cortex, the conscious part of our brain—'the high road' presence.

I didn't even have to think about it or feel it. In fact, I had an experience that I'll talk about in the next story that I had pushed down so far, it only surfaced a few years ago. This is how powerful the mind can be.

But remember, if we have the will (and that is the key) to push something away so much that we can't feel it, we most certainly have the will to change the way we talk and think about ourselves.

Getting to know the triune brain

Having spent many years investigating my own brain and trying to understand what was going on, this made so much sense to me. I hope that it can resonate with you and give you a better understanding of an incredibly powerful part of our own bodies that can be so overlooked.

The teachings of Dr Siegel helped me gain an understanding of what was actually going on when I was thinking a repetitive thought. Google *Hand Model of the Brain* for a visual on this.

The brain stem, limbic system and cortex all make up what is called the triune brain. This has developed in layers. The brain stem was the first to evolve (present in reptiles), then the limbic system (the mammalian brain), and last the cortex (developed in humans).

Integration of the brain means linking the activity and workings of these three areas. They all play a huge role in the balancing act of finding equilibrium in our nervous system.

Here is a short breakdown of the three:

Reptilian brain (brain stem)

- Fight, flight or freeze response
- Food, shelter, sex, digestion
- Basic functions of heart and lungs
- Autopilot

Mammalian brain (limbic system)

- Emotions, memories, habits, relationships (including ourselves)

- Safe or unsafe
- Fear response (amygdala)
- Determining right or wrong
- Reactive, not responsive

Human brain (cortex and neocortex, including the prefrontal cortex)

- Language, thought, choice, imagination, consciousness
- Rationality, research, reasoning
- Thinking about thinking
- Presence, awareness, creativity, intuition, imagination
- Willpower
- Response

Hopefully you can see that with a human brain, we are blessed with *choice*.

Practising perfection and searching for more leads to a habit of never being content with where we are at.

When we develop such a strong bunch of neurons, this firing and wiring becomes a very well-established pattern and then habit. We develop our program, or paradigm.

A paradigm can be many habits or beliefs that guide every move we make—affecting everything from our dialogue to how we view food, and the way we think we *should* look. It governs our communication, work ethics and how we see our success or failures.

Most of the time, your paradigms and belief systems didn't

originate with you. They were passed down from generations and through conditioning. Think of them as the accumulated practice of other people's habits, opinions and belief systems. They are the backbone of the driving belief in your life.

Negative paradigms and belief systems are the reason about ninety per cent of people in Western culture keep getting the same results day after day, year on year. Myself included.

Until the age of approximately seven, we are developing our 'programmed mind'. From then, if we don't consciously change our program (paradigm), it will be the same for our adult life.

I feel this quote from Chinese philosopher Lao-Tzu is appropriate here:

> Watch your thoughts; for they become your words.
> Watch your words; for they become your actions.
> Watch your actions; for they become your habits.
> Watch your habits; for they become your character.
> Watch your character; for that becomes your destiny.

My brain started to get used to the unkind words I would say to myself, the damaging thoughts I would think, and then of course the painful actions I would take over the next twenty-eight years of my life that eventually led me to find another way of being.

A desperate search for any other way to live.

It was the only real choice I had at the time, as I had once again entered into dangerous territory of suicidal thoughts, starving myself or heading back down the low road—the easy, numbing path.

We are not born perfectionists

I don't believe for one moment that perfectionism is a trait. In my eyes it's a learnt behaviour and very well practised, because possibly—and maybe this is true for you too—there is an underlying belief that we are not enough as we are.

So this constant chasing of perfection, stemming from the belief that I wasn't pretty, started to escalate on a bigger scale. A much bigger scale.

In time I realised that the ability to be my story and my light—and give others permission to recognise, accept and have gratitude for the skin we are in—was God's gift to me.

The spoilt brat

My younger, troubled self must have been a nightmare. I was super spoilt. I would bust at the seams when I didn't get what I wanted. I became quite demanding and ridiculously competitive, and I started to struggle in school. Well, in the things that 'mattered' of course. Maths, science and history delivered me less than average grades, but drama, art, hospitality and sport were my A game.

But what's an A game in creativity, when the system is based on your grades in maths or English?

That A game was dimmed by my own thoughts of *I wish I could just impress my family and have them proud of me.*

I was too busy chasing this and, of course, I felt like I was failing constantly at life. My childlike spark was getting darker and darker and I had no idea how to be myself. So I kept along the only road I knew—people pleasing and finding perfection the best I could so others would validate me and define my worth.

This is never, ever a good recipe for owning your authenticity.

Journal moment

Was there a time you spent living your life to please others? Maybe it's now?

How does the word 'people pleasing' sit with you?

Is it something where you are nodding your head like, Fuck yes, that's me all over?

I hear you. I get you. It's what we have been conditioned to do. And it's OK.

Let's get a little deeper on that. Why do you feel the need? What if you put that energy back into yourself? Does it feel good to people please when you would rather be saying, 'No, I have myself to put first'?

Take a look at nature for a moment. Everything is give and take, yin and yang, light and dark, effort and ease. We are exactly the same.

So if we are constantly pleasing others and our cup is not full, then how do we share the best we can? We must learn to put ourselves first.

Set those boundaries

This is not about not doing things for others. Doing things for others is our key to getting back. But choose to do things for others that also feel good for you. It's a no-brainer, it's effortless, and you don't go into it with the attitude of *I hope they appreciate my time doing this* or *I could have spent my time better today.*

If you don't want to do the thing, don't do the thing. Simple.

In the BE HERE method, the first thing discussed is our body. Your body will tell you if it's a big yes or not. In the BE

HERE method we start to learn to listen.

Learning to say no with a firm and decisive voice is one of the most empowering things you can do for yourself.

This constant drive to make others happy, unfortunately, is going to bring you to your knees. The tiredness you may already feel, the exhaustion, the fatigue, the stress, the bloating, the excess body weight, the shortness of patience, the lack of sleep, the need for more and the sense of *I have to* are all going to get too much one day and this is where you are going to have to make a choice.

Or you can choose to change it now.

Start to practise putting yourself first today. Do yoga, pause, go to the beach. Say no to a dinner outing if you would rather read, take a bath and nurture yourself. Stop trying to do everything to please others and start to watch your energy and self-worth shift.

The eating disorder choice

Smack bang in the middle of my teens, my perfectionism practice reached a new high. At the tender age of fifteen, I chose to not eat. That was the easiest way to chase perfection, right? I would choose to have the perfect body.

Well, I had two choices at the time, to be honest.

At fifteen I said '*Fuck* you life' and I flipped a coin.

I had been journalling dark thoughts for a while and had also been secretly cutting myself as I felt so unworthy and lacked the desire to live. I felt ashamed, guilty—yes, there is a sexual encounter here that I will unpack next—stupid and small and started to hate the way I looked. Remember, I wasn't 'pretty enough'.

This is a real letter my mum recovered from my dark days. I was about sixteen.

March 1998

Eat goddammit.
What's your problem? Think you'll get fat?
Ana.
Ana-rexic.
Ana-rex-ia. It even sounds evil.
Never thought that this was going to take a hold
of me.
Not a second time.
Speak of the devil.
I feel it now. It's coming, it's here.
Judgement, Blame, Shame.

Damn that Cornetto.
Damn that TV ad.
All those skinny chicks running around in cossies.
I wish I was that skinny.
I wish I had never met you.
But now you will be with me till I die.
So I suppose I had better start to like you.
Unless of course you keep doing that to me.

Mmm, smell that pizza.
I hope that bitch who eats that puts on twenty
kilos.

Dribbling on my single strawberry.
Save the other half for the rest of the day.
Eighty push-ups, ninety sit-ups, one-hundred leg
lifts and a thirty minute walk twice a day. What a
joke.
Look what you are doing to yourself.

No, it's alright, I'm not hungry.
Yes, I'm sure.
Go on … just one piece.
I swallow the chocolate.
Fat. Calories, sugar, fat, stomach, fat, things,
judgement, shame.
What a conscience.
Couldn't you have let me enjoy it for once?
Didn't think so.
I think I need to throw up.
Slam the toilet door shut … hang my head on the
side of the bowl so it's silent.
I've got it mastered now due to so much practice.
Now I feel satisfied.

What's wrong with you?
You've lost SO much weight.
You're so moody lately.
Hush … look how skinny she is.

Don't you think I know?
Don't you think I knew what would happen?
But I couldn't stop it. I just wanted more.
And it ate away at me.
It took my pride, my friends, my goals, my life.

I don't know who I am anymore.
Calorie and macro counting, burning fat,
minimising sugar.

Can't you see what you've done?
You have stolen me, and never will the real me
return.
It's happening all over again.
As much as I want to stop it, I can't.
I can see myself falling into your trap again.
But this time …
I don't think I'm going to crawl back out.

When I received this letter and others like it from my mum in August 2021, I cannot tell you just how proud I felt that I had come so far.

All eating disorders are behind me and it was my biggest gift to learn how to fall in love with myself.

I am beyond grateful for these letters because they remind me of how difficult it was at the time. I will never take any of it for granted.

The premiere of 'Ana'

As you may have come to realise, Ana is like a second person. The ego. The friend that you wish you never had. The constant chatter. The voice inside your head.

My first physical experience of anorexia struck at fifteen. The over-practised perfection, the tiresome people pleasing and the dull ring of thoughts of 'not enough' finally culminated in anorexia.

So one night at our family home at Kincumber, I had two things written down. 'Die' or 'starve'. I had been journalling for years many letters like the one you read above. It was a dark, grey and menacing world that I faced in my body.

And I had had enough.

Both seemed like reasonable options. What was I worth? I was now a timid, shy, competitive yet submissive teen who would do anything she could to be liked. And I was tired, over it, and disgusted by the person I seemed to be.

What other choice was available? Both seemed totally valid to that fifteen-year-old girl.

The coin flipped on tails. Starve.

The rest is history.

I'm so grateful it landed there, otherwise I would not be here sharing this story with kids and adults around the country, and practising kindness and compassion to myself.

This chasing of perfection of course became my learnt and practised pattern for nearly twenty-eight years. These thoughts and words were a by-product of energy that had been stored— the samskara—that I had of my own free will chosen not to move through. I had made those words my story and my label, and they ran my life.

Everything I did had to be perfect. And it started with the belief that I was not pretty enough right back at that tender, impressionable age of six. It did not start at fifteen.

It had grown like a volcano over those younger years. Nothing just happens.

Energy has to flow. When things are blocked and we continue to suppress them, we find they have to go somewhere. Mentally, physically and emotionally we start to fall apart, unless we allow ourselves to feel the pain and trauma we went through with compassion, and then move on from it. This is what this book is all about.

Years of blocked energy, along with a belief that I was not

enough, and a strong and determined practice of perfection and people pleasing… here we have the problem.

Over time, my brain was hardwired to numb and run, when I felt and experienced pain. Every time the samskaras were triggered—the experiences I pushed down or clung to—I tried my best to avoid or match these experiences. This is hard work and over twenty-five years becomes exhausting, tiring and mentally challenging. You lose your spark completely.

I went from a relatively healthy, sporty and competitive teen to a gaunt, sick, frail and very underweight version of myself who then became what I knew for the next quarter century of my life.

My eating disorder did not start at fifteen.

It started at the age of six.

This pain that was still sitting in my heart space—a samskara—drove deeper and deeper in, and every time it presented I pushed it back down aggressively. I chose to run more, swim more, exercise more, compete more and do more. This started the slow downward spiral of my health, my self-worth, my authenticity and my soul.

I had used my *will* to hold on to this. And it had to be my *will* to then do the work and land in a place of compassion and acceptance.

Your will is the strongest part of you and it's where the magic can happen.

The body's ability to heal

I hope this makes sense so far and I hope that it has you asking questions too about things that have happened in your life. Maybe people have said it's hereditary, or 'we are really not sure how it started.'

Maybe you have heard the news, 'These things just happen' or 'You're one of the small number of the population who this happens to.' And probably the worst that many anorexia or eating disorder sufferers face: 'Once you have an eating disorder, you always will.'

I made this my story, my label, and it defined me for nearly fifteen years, until I learnt that I had the ability, with my thoughts and words, to change my story. You can too.

This is not just about eating disorders.

My mother was told she had three weeks left to live when she was delivered her ovarian cancer diagnosis.

She is still here with us today, after also receiving the diagnosis of breast cancer. She chose not to believe it deep down. Her *will* to live outweighed the words of someone else.

My mother's drive to beat her diagnosis still rocks me to this day. She had a wisdom deep within her that knew she could turn it around … and that she did. She is a powerful, determined and courageous woman who I think is still unsure of just how much strength and courage she manifested to still be with us today.

Mum, you have no idea how much this time in your life shaped my own. It gave me the desire to see what I could do, rather than what I could not. Though I didn't realise it at the time, your strength left a deep-rooted message in me that with my will, I could create the life of my dreams. We all do. As you taught me, it comes down to believing that you can.

When we are told a diagnosis or a timeline of what is left of our life, or what to expect, this can either go one of two ways. We either take it as our label (as I did) or choose to be the creator of our reality from this moment forward, or at least give it a shot. Know that whatever you, your children or your family are told, nothing is permanent; I believe all can be changed in your mind and your body (unless it is physical trauma).

Anne

I witnessed only recently how powerful our minds can be with a beautiful woman and dear friend I met in the Hunter Valley.

With the power of her mind, Anne decided that she was going to heal her body from the inside out. Suffering from damage to sixty per cent of her liver, she was not a great state, but I knew upon speaking with her that she was not done; she was in search of guidance from God as to how she would change her story.

After three months in isolation and being in nature, Anne was able to pause, to feel and experience her emotions and stored trauma. She was able to access her deep wounds and finally feel them. When the doctors came to check on her liver health and performed blood tests, they were dumbfounded to report that the tests deemed her one hundred per cent clear of cirrhosis.

This is just not possible. Or is it?

Anne accessed something much deeper than the physical self in that time. She tapped into her spiritual being and the *belief* that healing was a possibility. She did not once waver from that and she has been given a beautiful gift from the Universe. She can now pay her message forward.

It's worth noting here that the gentleman who has stolen my heart for many years—the rocker, the legend, the long-haired loose-as-fuck gentle giant with the blue guitar ... Dave Grohl—also speaks on this 'belief' on page 62 of his incredible book *The Storyteller.*

The why behind the words

Over three and a half years ago, I had a dream that I would create a book sharing the words, practices and advice that helped me move from nearly thirty years of self-sabotage, judgement, comparison and unworthiness to acceptance and self-compassion. I visualised what it would look like. I felt into who I was speaking to and how it would make them feel when they put these practices into place. And I imagined, and believed, like nothing else, that the words from this book *Watch YA Language* would hit home to those who needed it the most.

In 2019, I physically created my own book and placed it in my bookshelf so it would sit there each day and stare back at me and remind me of my dream. To never EVER lose sight of the intention and the *why* behind these words. To live each day true to my heart, my intuition and the belief that I damn well could.

And here we are.

You can change the story

If you have ever been told 'We don't know why this happens' or 'It just happens in some people,' I say bullshit.

In my experience with others, and from years of research into trauma, addictions and behaviours, I know there is always something deep down. You may not know it yet. Be patient with your unravelling. It takes time, but there would have been a moment of pain or trauma likely when you were a kid that has stuck, gone deep into the heart and been buried for however long.

This is now a practice of compassion. I understand that some of these words are not going to be warm and fuzzy. In fact, they may well be downright triggering. But I gently want to remind you to sit with it with kindness.

Remember, use your triggers as your teachers.

They may bring up pain, anger and resentment, and you might even feel yourself starting to close and get a little frustrated.

Don't run from or numb them. We all know this gets us

nowhere fast.

Being triggered is not a bad thing. I see 'trigger warnings' all over the place. In my eyes, a trigger warning is a great opportunity to bring up the stuff—the samskaras, the things that have caused pain and are blocking our energy—so it can be felt and allowed to heal. If you avoid something due to a trigger warning, you are going to choose to avoid it for many years to come and it is going to be harder and harder to face when you get older. Remember the story of my dear nan? Don't let yourself hold on to the stuff.

Nothing in this world is worth holding on to. You have held on to it long enough.

If by chance any of that is happening, gently thank yourself for feeling. There is obviously something there that is needing to be addressed and heard, otherwise you would be breezing over this stuff with no reaction at all.

When you feel this tension and your body starts to close, remember this quote from Michael Singer's *The Untethered Soul*: 'Nothing, ever, is worth closing your heart over.'

A little introduction to the BE HERE method

Can you allow yourself to feel, to heal?

The BE HERE method truly was a huge part of my own waking up and realising I could choose to offer myself kindness and compassion, whereas before I would talk to myself like shit, roll in self-sabotage and hate and repeat negative thoughts over and over.

Kindness generates gratitude.

This method is the lessons from many of my mentors and teachers, my parents, my nan and friends and strangers who have helped me to feel all my emotions, and become curious about what they can teach me.

This method, to this day, brings me back to the here and now. In the present moment, I can make a choice. So can you.

Information is never owned. I believe it is shared.

You can download the ebook of the method from my website at watchyalanguage.com.

Body

The first tool we have is recognising somatically when we have been triggered.

Our shoulders tense, our heart closes, our body heats up, we get short of breath, our tummy bloats.

Repeat this often when you feel a shift: 'I see you, body.'

Emotion

When we are triggered, we first feel our bodies react and I guarantee you there is an emotion behind the tension.

Call it out to yourself. 'I am *experiencing* judgement. I am *choosing* to compare. I am *deciding* to put myself down. I am finding this *really hard* right now.' Whatever it is, become aware of the thought and the words you are saying to yourself. It is only from here you can do something about it and start to change your brain.

Notice the emphasis on the example provided. We are not our thoughts, and we are not our heart. We are the ones who *experience* the thoughts and the emotions. (More on this later.)

Call it out in the mind. Anxiety, fear, doubt, worry, small, unsafe, judging.

Call it out in the body. Tight, tense, blocked, bloated, locked up, closed, sick, stuck.

Say, 'I see you, I feel you, and it's OK.'

Heart

What is it that I *need* right now?

Often, we feel the challenging emotion and then we push it away, thinking we shouldn't be feeling it. *I'm a bad person or I'm feeling guilty because of X.* What if you just allowed the anxiety, allowed the judging, allowed the blame, the shame, the guilt, the fear, the doubt and the pain. Let it be. Let it sit. Let it be there. With compassion. You will then yield to what is. You will drop the fight of trying to make it right, trying to push it away, trying to change it or resist it. This saves so much energy.

Surrender.

Nurture what is here right now for you. Surrender to the discomfort and give yourself permission to allow it with kindness. Be a kind human. Not just to others, but to yourself. You have a choice.

American self-help and spiritual author Wayne Dyer once said: 'If you change the way you look at things, the things you look at change.' We have a choice in how we respond to every single situation. Some situations are horrible and others are deliciously pleasant and euphoric. All situations are meant to be felt, experienced, lived in the moment and then allowed to pass through us. Be kind to you here.

Dance. Sing. Move. Cry. Cuddle your dog. Have sex. Cook. Clean. Get a facial. Move. Rest. Do whatever it takes to receive. We are in a society that finds it so hard to receive. Receive the love your inner child needs here. Ask the question, *What is it that I need right now?* and go do that.

Empower

Learn! Continue to learn. Face discomfort every day. Get to know your brain and nervous system, and above all, start to use your biggest teacher, your body. It is *always* talking to you and your gut is the answer to everything you need to know.

Our bodies talk to us *all the time*. Inflammation, injury, sickness, disease, bloating and digestive issues are all cues from our bodies to *tune in* and listen.

A bandaid solution will only get us so far and not heal the root of the problem.

Respond. Don't react.

Ninety-nine per cent of the time, whatever is unfolding in front of you *will unfold anyway*. This step reminds you that you have a choice as to how much of your attention and energy you give to a situation. I guarantee you that reading a comment on social media, losing your keys, running late for work or missing the bus is absolutely no reason to react and put your nervous system into fight-or-flight. This will only cause havoc on your digestion. You know the deal. Things get stuck.

Reactivity can stem from lack of self-care, poor sleep, minimal movement, food choices that are processed or low in nutrients, and high stress/busyness/overwhelm. Reactivity can be likened or related to the limbic (emotional) brain and (overactive) amygdala.

Response is present, aware and thoughtful. It is making the choice to let go, walk away and choose to disengage. It comes from the part of our brain that we as humans are blessed with, our prefrontal cortex, the place that allows us to think about thinking, explore imagination, indulge in creativity and have a choice.

Energy

In practising the prior steps, we start to change our energy and vibration. By becoming present (being here), and being the witness of what is going on, we are able to use our willpower to make a choice as to how we move through our days. The practice of presence starts to create a different experience, and we move from autopilot to aware. This is when we create neuroplasticity, and chemically change our brain, and physiologically change our bodies.

When our energy changes, we vibrate on a higher level and start to show up as our best self, and the Universe starts to deliver. Remember that God is only giving us what we are asking for—positive or negative.

The heart is the creator of our emotions. Emotions are a vibration. Vibrations are energy and when we change our energy, we start to attract the vibrational match for what we are thinking and feeling. I'll talk about this more in the last story.

The practice of this method is with me often. I work on and repeat these steps every single damn day.

Again, kindness generates gratitude.

Whatever you do, don't close.

Our hearts are meant to feel. They are meant to vibrate with emotion. We are always experiencing. Nothing is meant to be stored there. The reason we store our stuff is that we have clung to or resisted a moment that has happened in the past. Hopefully this is making a little more sense now.

A closed heart can generate all kinds of physical and emotional issues in the body, such as:

- lung and breathing problems
- high blood pressure

- chest or upper back pain
- breast complications
- arm, elbow and hand ailments
- inability to receive love for the self
- lack of self-compassion
- tight shoulders and traps, hunched inwards

I'm so grateful that I can now cry and express emotions freely. I never used to. I didn't know how. I had stuffed my feelings so deeply down that all I knew was how to be strong, stoic, rigid and unemotional. It still blows me away that I am writing these words today and in the space that I am. We can only change these pathways when we are open to change.

I had to become the observer of my own words, behaviours and thoughts to become present enough to change them with my will, repetition and a belief that I could.

I spent many years caught up in my own world that was very closed, unresponsive and small. I wasn't able to see the big picture and thought everyone and everything was out to get me. That was my reality. That was the energy I was creating.

I know Nan is watching over me in each moment. Every time I see a white butterfly I feel her presence, and I know she would be so proud of me for writing this book, for staying true to my heart, for trusting my gut and speaking my truth. Each time I close, I think of her and do my best to not hold on to any moments, feel what I need to feel and let go.

It has been a practice, and it will always be a practice for me to be as open, curious and expansive as possible. To see the lesson in the chaos, receive the blessing in the darkness and choose to have gratitude for the moments that rock me to my core. With practice, and now firm belief and excitement, I know I have the opportunity to see what I wish to see and create what I truly want.

The push for more

Let's come back to the story of fifteen-year-old me, awkward, shy and now increasingly anxious as I continued to spiral to a darker place. My drive for life became even more dull. My competitive side, and my pushy, stubborn, fast persona all started to melt away, physically and mentally. I continued to swim but lost my drive. My world seemed pointless and I even lost any belief in myself that I was worthy of competing.

The letters I mentioned near the beginning of this story were written in my darkest of days. I don't remember a thing and they show just how wrapped up I was in the double-edged sword (and personality) that is Ana. I could not be more grateful for the return of these letters; I know that they were so necessary for where my life is now, as I move forward to work with kids and adults who are still battling these demons.

When you have nothing left

At fifteen, a body-conscious, long-legged, anxious and timid version of myself stepped up to the blocks at Homebush for the national trials. Back in the day, as mentioned, I was competing against swimmers such as Leisel Jones. Reading her biography, I found out she had a similar battle with the same feelings as me. Leisel's road took her to anxiety and depression, but the core is the same—a deep sense of not ever being enough and constant striving for more.

As I stood on the blocks, on the verge of being diagnosed with glandular fever, I remember thinking, *I'm done. I'm tired, I'm shattered, and I don't want to do this anymore.*

I simply stepped off before my qualifier and stood down. My coaches and mum stood up and threw their arms up in the air, and all I heard was silence. The dead, numb and eerie silence of a dark and dismal spiral that was about to follow my choice.

As I mentioned in Story One, there was another feeling that only solidified my belief of my body not being perfect. As we were standing in the stalls, one of the other competitors in line had compared my thighs to hers.

'Your thighs are thicker than mine,' she said. Nonchalantly, not knowing how deep that statement cut like a knife, ripping open those old scars of that deflated six-year-old and the old story of 'not feeling pretty enough.'

Hopefully you are getting an idea on how these samskaras are built over the years and how we hold on to them so tightly that they become us … if we let them.

So I stepped down off the blocks. Only this time, not for a challenge of fitness, swimming or competing. It was to be a perfectionist at having an eating disorder, because that's what I could control.

The determination was back. The spark, the drive and the competition. But not for a good reason. The goal now was to get thin. Very thin.

Because when I am thin and have small thighs, I'll be liked, right? I will be perfect and it will be OK.

I was so wrong.

A label allows us to play victim

A few months later, aged sixteen, I was skin and bones at Gosford Hospital. At thirty-six kilos, I imagine I wasn't a pleasant sight. I blamed others for my situation and refused to take responsibility.

I was sitting in the dietician's office. Soft hair covered my entire body and I had constant goosebumps because I was always cold. My belly felt hard. I could feel my ribs every time I breathed a short, almost forced breath. I had developed a terrible nervous habit of biting the inside of my mouth, along with chewing my fingernails. I sat there curled in a hopeless mess. My head hung heavy over a body that was way too small for my age.

The crisp and curt short-haired woman walked in, looked me up and down, and without hesitation went through the 'standard' put-on-weight-quick system, and said that if I didn't do it, I would die. She labelled me with a mental health condition that I then decided to use as my excuse, my label, my life for nearly two decades.

Upon hearing the words, 'Once you have an eating disorder, you always will,' I believed that I would never heal from it, so my brain was like *Fuck it all. Let's just get wasted, stay skinny.* I decided to take whatever I could to numb the pain.

It's also worth noting here that the slow decline of my mental health matched the darkness of my thoughts and words. I unconsciously was creating more of the same, and no matter how much I wanted change, I didn't realise that my dialogue and thoughts played the starring role in this particularly long groundhog day.

The chase for perfection, however, got stronger and stronger as I moved from anorexia to a 'stable weight' and into a bulimia journey that took me through my twenties and early thirties.

And so it began

In the low, distant, sad and vulnerable state I was in, of course I believed the dietitian. I became the victim of that story. I am not dismissing the help good dietitians can provide, however it wasn't appropriate for my healing of the deeper wound that was calling for the work to come from the inside out.

I was given some food advice based on the pyramid, a certain number of calories to hit (an exessive amount of processed food for someone just revisiting and relearning how to eat) and an absolute no for exercise or movement, which when I look back on it now, was a recipe for disaster.

I feel we are missing an absolute vital point: how to listen to the body. Educating myself on dismissing the diet culture; preparing and eating your food with love and not fear; noticing how food makes you feel; listening to your body; moving to feel good, not to punish; and learning to understand when your body is in fight-or-flight was my recipe for healing my wounds.

I highly recommend diving into the study of Ayurveda. The two main concepts of this ancient science are that:

1. The body and mind are connected
2. Nothing has more power to heal the body than the mind

This practice is a huge part of my life today and always will be.

Funnily enough, Ayurveda and movement is now my area of expertise. In 2021, I started to bring together the immersive experience of healing from the inside out. I share teachings of movement, Ayurveda and somatic awareness (how to recognise tension and when we are living in overdrive), and the tools that have helped me unravel the layers and give back to the world (my *dharma*). This is done both online and in Newcastle, with workshops set to be extending out Australia-wide by the end of 2022.

I feel so grateful for this opportunity; everything is unfolding in divine time. You can stay up to date with the Watch YA Language and The Perfection Pandemic workshops over on my website at watchyalanguage.com or my Instagram page @watch. ya.language.

A broken record of belief

So in this tender, and very vulnerable state, here I was—a victim to blame, and a victim of the Universe serving a shitty hand at life. Never did I even think to look at my own choices and decisions or take ownership of where I was until my mid-thirties.

Never, until I dived in to do the work, did I believe that with my words, I could heal my body.

Be careful what you choose to believe.

On a side note, it can be a similar situation with the medical industry and diagnosis.

'You have cancer.'

'You have endometriosis.'

'You have an autoimmune disease.'

'You have PCOS.'

'You'll never walk again.'

'You're obese.'

'You have a condition that needs treatment and drugs for the rest of your life.'

'You have a condition that has now been labelled.' We fall victim to that label if we so choose to.

In my opinion and from my research, our cells are changing constantly and renewing until we die. This is the research and study of neuroplasticity. It proves that what fires together, wires together, and if we keep repeating the same thoughts, words, choices, actions, behaviours and experiences, we will have the same emotions.

These emotions—energy in motion—repeat the same thoughts over and over.

The only way to change ourselves chemically in the brain and biologically in the body is to create a different thought, which sparks different words, choices, actions, behaviours and experiences. In turn, this gives us a new emotion. It is that new emotion—remember it comes from the heart—that starts to change our way of being: brain and body.

More on this can be found in chapter three of Dr Joe Dispenza's book *You Are the Placebo*.

Again, in my eyes, we can always do something about the current state we are in to help ourselves find better health. Energy is everything and when we practise more compassion, gratitude and kindness, we are sending out a message to the Universe that this is what we want more of back at us.

I believe that getting to know our brain, and the state of our nervous system, is the key to the tools we need to move forward from whatever patterns and habits we have created. You are the only one who can invite yourself to change.

The BE HERE method allows you to become present in the moment that's unfolding, relax and loosen your body, open your heart and make a choice whether you are going to react with the old, practised habits and dialogue, or respond with compassion and acceptance. It is only from presence that we are able to choose a new thought, new words and a new way of being.

Then we need to practise the shit out of that.

By choosing the latter we create a different experience, and it's that experience, when practised consistently, that changes our language for good.

There is much more research in the books I have mentioned on the way in which neuroplasticity and different thought patterns have altered people's physical, mental, and emotional health. This includes healing autoimmune diseases, sleep disorders, ADHD, cancers and more, just by changing the way people think and feel.

The ABC reported in 2015:

Scientists now know that the brain has an amazing ability to change and heal itself in response to mental experience. This phenomenon, known as neuroplasticity, is considered to be one of the most important developments in modern science for our understanding of the brain.

We can all change

When someone labels you by saying, 'You have [insert condition here],' they make you the victim of the story. My research shows that these words, labels and systems are common in the rigid recovery systems of today. I also believe these are some of the most damaging and darkest words you can hear when you are as low as I was.

So there started my 'recovery' as such. To put on weight, I was force-fed 'calories' that were processed, unnatural and downright toxic. Things such as chocolate bars, white bread, high-sugar cereals and fizzy drinks were in my 'healing program'.

I was never taught to understand or get to know food as a friend, to eat it slowly and with love and compassion. I was never once taught how to listen to my body and tune in when things started to show up. I just ignored them and soldiered on.

Slowly, over time, the wheels started to fall off.

Please hold no judgement here on yourself or others for their own journey with food, upbringing or choices along the way. We are all just doing the best we can with the information we know. When we know, we can do better.

With my clients, that is exactly where I start. As it *all* starts from there.

We've all heard the old adage 'Food is medicine.'

If we are only taught to eat and drink sugar from a place of being severely unwell and undernourished, then we are just placing a bandaid over the problem, and years down the track, when a healthier weight is reached, we will not have the tools to make good and intuitive choices with food. We have seen in many cases how this lack of understanding and listening to the body spirals decades later into poor food choices and an unhealthy relationship with food, dialogue and body.

My dream is to facilitate a hub in Australia to combat what I call The Perfection Pandemic. In this space, both teens and adults would be free to move, breathe, and learn how to listen to their bodies and shift their shitty self-talk from judgement and comparison to compassion and kindness.

I want people to build a new relationship with food, treating it as a friend rather than foe. My desire is for people to embrace authenticity and let go of perfection. The hub will be a place where individuals can practise movement, play and fall in love with themselves all over again.

Movement changed my life. I have been a personal trainer since nineteen, but the practice of movement, getting to know my body and getting to know how I intuitively respond to different things taught me the goodness I never ever thought I would learn. The humbling practice of learning to do a handstand, use gymnastics rings, crawl, cartwheel, backbend, play and connect with others was a game changer, letting me let go of the 'goal' and appreciate the moment for however imperfect it is, without the need for more. Hence why I believe this is an important part of anyone's self-growth.

The more we learn, the less we know. Our bodies were born to move. Exercise is a modern-day word and movement is what we were born to do. Play is something we never lose, unless we decide to.

Movement is not exercise. It is what we are born to do.

We have a body. It needs to be looked after from the inside

out. It is not meant to be on the go all the time and sweat does not equal results. Like nature we must find duality, the fast with the slow, the supple with the strong and the yin within the yang.

If you are still going to the gym to burn off last night's meal, you are heading down a hamster wheel of destruction.

So for me, sharing this beautiful practice of movement with whoever I can gets me so damn excited!

My intention is to encourage people to appreciate where they are, rather than think *When I get X I'll be happy.* To have fun, become strong and supple, be faced with discomfort, learn and use the brain every day. To play more, laugh often and stop searching for more.

I have no doubt this will happen one day for many humans, and it lights me up just to think about it. I will not stop until I've done all I can to shift our dialogue from judgement and comparison to acceptance and self-compassion.

A sinking ship

It's important to mention here that while I was slowly tearing myself apart, those closest to me were also being pulled with me.

The pain, suffering and grief that I put my family through I can't even begin to explain. I don't feel guilt or shame for it anymore. I did.

I let that go quite a few years ago. Mind you, I spent many years blaming myself for how they suffered due to my illness.

I now have a bigger understanding that it was what it was and it was all part of the process. It's not worth hanging on to what happened. What matters is right now. We have this moment.

Danny Abdallah is such a great teacher of how we can remain present and compassionate, and do our best to stay open.

On a side note, if you are struggling with an eating disorder or have a child who is, the game is changing now and a more holistic, real and gentle approach is being taken. There are more studies available on brain patterns and habits, and eating disorder origins, and more evidence of links to trauma or pain as a young child, rather than the old *Oh, it runs in the family* or *These things just happen* stories.

It is also important to note our own patterns and behaviours, thoughts and words around our kids. Children and animals are huge receivers of energy and can tell when you limit your food because you are punishing your body for what you ate yesterday, or tear apart your thighs and tummy in the mirror. They are always watching.

I understand that I have dived quite deep into that part of the perfection journey: the constant chase for more. I have shared from my experience, however it's not just eating disorders that have us striving rather than arriving. It's also pressure from sport, expectations that we grow up with, social media and body image, family traditions, religion, values, beliefs and conditioning that can have us stuck in repetitive and familiar patterns of behaviours, thoughts, actions and addictions.

Do you still blame yourself for the actions of others or yourself? Is this really serving you? What would it feel like to free yourself of this?

I'm going to be very, very blunt. Please know that the energy behind these words and stories comes only from a place of love. I share them with a deep-rooted intention to help you, the reader, heal yourself so that you can be the light for your children and then their own.

If you are a parent and find that you are holding on to guilt of the past from whatever happened however long ago, it is only going to be stored in your body, and I promise you that right now, at this moment, it is totally irrelevant. If we choose to hold on and let this guilt run (or ruin) the rest of our lives, is it possible that these patterns will be passed down to our kids.

In later stories, I share some more teachings from Dr Daniel Siegel, as well as from Dr Tina Payne Bryson. (And no, I am not a parent of a human child; I have a very cute, protective but loving fur baby, Lilly, who is a devoted grand-dog to my folks, but my work draws me to the kids of our future.) I find their book to be one of the best in the field: *The Power of Showing Up*. This not only has helped me understand my own avoidance patterns, but also, with compassion, the history of my upbringing—without judgement.

Healing trauma is a slow but rewarding journey. Choosing to keep it stored in our subconscious is a minefield for inflammation, sickness and dis-ease. The work will be presented to you when you are ready. This is not something to be rushed or pushed. Seek help, speak out, talk with those you trust: just be open as to how your healing will occur and you will be guided in divine timing. Figuring out the how is not our job ... that's up to God.

This holding on is fear. Fear of not being seen, fear of not being heard, fear of who we might be if others knew of our suffering or past, and the big fear of not being enough. This energy of fear manifests into physical illness. I stand by this and have witnessed it. My own body withheld fear, anger, guilt and shame for over two decades; my choice to change my dialogue and thoughts created the pause I needed in my neural pathways to give my brain the opportunity to rewire.

I recommend investigating on your own healing journey the teachings of Dr John Sarno along with the principles of Ayurveda and Eastern medicine.

If you visit the video 'How to Release Guilt. A mother's advice on kids with Eating Disorders' on my YouTube account, you will hear from my mum how long she held on to the guilt.

Again, this is not just for eating disorders. Maybe you feel guilt or blame for something that has happened along the way.

Whatever you did, whatever choice you made, you were doing your best with the information you had. We all have a choice, as I did, whether we put ourselves through painful experiences. No amount of holding on to what you should have said, could have done or would have liked to have done, and no matter how much you wished it were different is going to change the outcome. You need to start delivering this energy, attention and compassion back into you. You can only *show*, not *tell*.

Whatever is done is done.

You have held on to those thoughts and ways of thinking long enough, right?

Stop trying to fix it. It is what it is. Again, if we are holding on to this, we are thinking there is something wrong with us, that we are not enough, that we made poor decisions and don't deserve compassion or joy for ourselves.

Truth bomb. When you choose to believe this about yourself, you are just living in your own pity party and allowing yourself to be a victim of your own words.

Yes, this may be a harsh reality to hear, but I've been there and done that for more than twenty-eight years and all I did was create more of the same. I don't wish that on anyone.

It's now time to be kind. To slowly start to give yourself permission to receive.

You are worthy of feeling good. So am I.
That was always the story.

Instead of fighting it any longer, facing each day with the should haves, could haves and would haves, try leaving it as is and focusing on how you can now put that energy of worry, blame, shame, guilt and self-doubt into yourself in more positive forms. Lift yourself up. We have a choice.

If you are struggling letting this go, check in with my meditations in the Resources section at the end of this book. Or, over on my website watchyalanguage.com you can find access to my current online courses.

Uncovery to recovery

Upon finishing this book there were some amazing things that just fell into place. That's what happens when you are in flow.

When we understand that we have made a choice somewhere along the way as to how we have responded to certain situations, environments and people, we start to take ownership of our own actions. It's here where we can heal the deep scars that have possibly started the early onset of an eating disorder or mental illness.

Again, this is just my opinion and experience as someone who has been there and lived through it. I do encourage you to do your research, and it starts by getting to understand and know yourself and not take everything you hear at face value. This can also be applied to what we are experiencing in the world right now with the unfolding pandemic.

Do your own research from all angles. Be open and curious about everything. Listen to what your body tells you. You wouldn't just buy the first couch you sat on, so also don't take the first piece of advice you are told, no matter who it's from— including me.

Remember that all hospitals are there to provide a great job, however they are funded by the drug industry and medications are dished out like lollies in a lolly shop. The more we take them, the more we numb the feelings, and what we practise gets stronger.

I'm not saying medication is unnecessary. I fully and wholly believe drugs are useful for a certain amount of time until we can pause, feel better, start to regulate our nervous system and find a state of equilibrium in our body and mind.

Our bodies have every single tool in the shed to heal themselves. It starts with calming down our digestive and nervous systems. We will only remain in ill health if we are living in constant fight or flight.

Taking medication is needed in many circumstances—I was medicated also for a while—but it is just a bridge in the road, not a solution for the rest of our lives. We need to understand the core of the problem, and in my eyes, that means unlocking the layers we have created over our true selves—these samskaras we have either resisted or clung to.

Do the work. Get real with yourself and get to understand what's underneath. Get curious, not critical about what shows up. You may as well. Whatever is going to show up will show up anyway. Your choice is to move through it with curiosity and see how you can find ease.

It's not fun. It can be completely terrifying, but it's even more terrifying to spend your life avoiding the pain or triggers that can be anywhere anytime, which takes precious energy every day and will eventually pull you down, dim your light and have you feeling a fraction of the being that you are.

Practising perfection not only took over my life, but became me. I lost my whole sense of self and belonging as I became too caught up in what everyone else thought of me.

I only use an eating disorder as an example, as of course this was my ride, but I believe there is still an underlying belief when dealing with depression, post-traumatic stress disorder, anxiety and other mental illnesses that we are not enough as we are, and that we must constantly search for something more (which, of course, we will never find).

Bessel van der Kolk states in *The Body Keeps the Score*:

> Traumatised people chronically feel unsafe inside their bodies: The past is alive in the form of gnawing interior discomfort. Their bodies are constantly bombarded by visceral warning signs, and, in an attempt to control these processes, they often become expert at ignoring their gut feelings and in numbing awareness of what is played out inside. They learn to hide from their selves.

A samskara—energy that has been resisted or clung to.

I'm hoping the penny is starting to drop here. If we suppress the feelings and emotions that we experienced in a certain moment and hold on to them in the hope that they will go away, they will manifest as blockages in the physical body.

Finally, perfection can look like so many things but we rarely are aware that we are practising it.

I worried about my hair and got angry if it was out of place. I would body- and mirror-check so often it made me anxious. These days people use their phone. I constantly checked how my body looked to others, what car I drove, how much money I had in the bank, what others would think if I said or did this or that, what impression I would leave with new people. I even worried about what I would do for a living, making sure I was fitting the standard set by society.

This takes so much energy above anything else and if we can see this from an observer's point of view, we are trying to adapt ourselves to fit the mould of who we think we should be in society.

Oh? You're nodding your head? Have you too felt the need

to fit into society, your parents', teachers' or coaches' dreams of who you are meant to be? An expectation that others have put on you, a belief that whatever you do is not enough? What label you have to carry to be accepted, how you have to look and act for others.

Does it exhaust you? Yup, it exhausts me too.

When I'm out of alignment and living in fear, I fall straight back into these expectations, old beliefs and conditioning. That's when I come back to the BE HERE method to bring me to presence so I can choose again.

Do we all feel this way? This might be a great opportunity to journal and release.

Conditioning

Conditioning is something we have all been a part of, and always will be. However, we can always choose what we take on board once we become present and can intuitively feel what feels right or wrong for us.

This can be attributed to many factors: how we are raised (and how our parents or carers were raised), what we are shown as little kids (monkey see, monkey do), advertising, shopfronts, billboards, influencers, gym campaigns (you know, the summer body or bikini body challenges for guys and girls). The things we felt we had to hold back, like playfulness and creativity, for fear of being laughed at or judged. Little girls are seen and not heard.

I also feel it's very much due to the competitive nature of always trying to do better. Since school we are taught we have to strive to achieve a grade, to be the top of the class, to be the best. We are placed in first, second or third. We are celebrated for the wins and given medals and awards when we 'please the teachers', so we try to be the teacher's pet.

After school, this conditioning doesn't change much. We're into the workplace and we battle again with bullying, comparison, competition and the ever-long battle of 'climbing the ladder', which always comes with more work, more stress, more labels. And there's the constant need for and addiction to more: more wealth, more status, more labels, more things.

Perfection in my eyes is to fit a mould of other people's and society's expectations of us. To never be content with where we are at.

I could write a book on this as well: as I do my final edit on this book, I have actually already started. Hopefully you can see how our early conditioning, patterns and teachings play a huge role in developing our sense of self and who we think we need to be.

Hopefully you can also see that if we have impressions stored in us about who we think we should be, a label we carry or a limiting belief or trauma that we have resisted and pushed away, our chase for improvement will control us for the rest of our lives unless we recognise what's going on and do things to start to change it.

Again, it's so important to stress that the people who raise us—parents, carers, grandparents, friends or whoever is our 'family'—in most cases, are doing the best with what they know from a place of love and kindness.

Remember, they have also been taught by their parents, and so on. These patterns are well ingrained and practised for decades in the home, and in society. There is no right or wrong: it just is.

They likely struggled with their own perfectionism, people pleasing and expectation battles just like you or me. Offer compassion and love only and give out what you would like to receive back.

You were not born this way. None of us were.

What is learned can be unlearned. You are not what you think defines you. The labels you have placed on yourself are self-created and irrelevant now. You were not born with them.

Just as you were not born a perfectionist. Really. It doesn't matter if your mum or dad was one (or thought they were). You still have a choice. Remember, just as we can hold on to past events, with our willpower we can choose to practice perfection … just like I did for so many years. So with our willpower, we are able to start to change it! Let that sink in for a moment as you let a big sigh out.

You have a choice to continue to run from these impressions the rest of your life, or get a little uncomfortable.

You may choose to avoid situations that make you feel uncomfortable, such as confronting your fears, standing up and sharing your story or idea, breaking up with the partner who just pulls you down, or doing the thing that your heart has desired for so long. You may voice your opinion, you may choose to embrace your sexuality, you might even change who you are to suit you rather than everyone else.

And yes, it's terrifying.

But how would it feel to be trapped by your fears, your trauma, your impressions for the rest of your life?

If you choose to do this and just settle into a ho-hum kinda lifestyle where you feel tired, blah, stressed, exhausted, lacking in energy and vitality and really have no direction in life or drive, you will spend the rest of your days avoiding any situations that will push your buttons or bring up these held-down emotions and feelings.

That's up to you.

Or, maybe your work is now to start to ask why.

Why do I feel the need to be perfect here?

Why do I constantly think my body needs to look like this?

Why am I constantly judging or comparing myself to others?

Why do I not feel enough?

This is a lifetime of work, so be gentle, take your time. Don't force the answers; they will come. This is where the BE HERE method comes into play. To *finally* start to get to know you from the inside out with curiosity, not criticism.

Can I drop a little secret? I believe many of us travel through the 'not enough' story at some time in our lives or have felt a sense of lack or longing, or the need to be more or do more.

But everything in nature is accomplished, yet nothing is forced. Let your journey of you be the same.

Surrender to what is—how your body is, what you do, where you are at, how much money you have in the bank—and you start to not give a flying fuck what others think of you. You now have your starting point for embracing and empowering your higher self.

Don't compare yourself to others.

Don't compare it to what you see on social media.

Don't compare it to where you were.

Meet yourself where you are at. Right here. Without the need to fix, without the thought of *I'll be happy when* ... without the expectation of being anywhere else but here.

Have gratitude and appreciation for all that you have right now. Your body is an incredible vehicle within which you can go places, move, breathe, play, explore, create, be still, live and be. You are amazing just as you are.

This is it. We have right now, especially with COVID-19. I believe it's teaching us so much about being present and living in this moment and really diving into where we are at right now, without the need for more.

Practise the art of being imperfect. When you have appreciation for what's already here, more of that will come back to you and every single part of your being will grow. You will become more abundant, and have more energy and vitality. You will start to glow with a light that reflects acceptance and contentment. And that will be your gift to others; you will inspire them to do the same and practise imperfection too.

Today, catch yourself trying to strive. Thinking that you'll be better when you lose ten kilograms, get that pesky yoga pose or headstand you have been working on, fit into that dress, nail the perfect partner, burn a certain amount of calories, land the perfect job or get your next degree. Can you be utterly content with and accepting of what is right in front of you?

And then practise that every moment.

What you practise grows stronger.

Journal moment

- What is it that I find myself constantly striving for?
- How does that feel in my body?
- Is there anything for which I am constantly searching?
- What if I could lean in to the idea that my life is imperfectly perfect just as it is now?
- What does that feeling look like in my body?
- What can I tell myself each morning in the mirror that makes me feel good?

If with our willpower and choice we have got ourselves here, then it is with our willpower and choice that we can choose to live a life full of gratitude, love and acceptance.

SHAME, GUILT, JUDGEMENT AND THE BLAME GAME

What we resist persists

Only a few years ago I was walking barefoot along Bar Beach in Newcastle listening to a School of Greatness podcast episode from Lewis Howes on the sexual trauma he experienced as a child. I had just finished yoga.

It was two years after a life-changing trip to Bali and I had really started learning from my yoga teachings about getting curious about the things I was doing, saying, choosing, and believing about myself.

I had started to slowly do the work, and they say that God only gives you what you can handle.

I walked slowly on this truly magical Newie day. My feet dragged in the water as I tuned in and out of this podcast.

About twenty minutes in, Howes said some words that stopped me in my tracks: 'I chose to hide this sexual trauma away, and being a man, it was easier to bottle it up and not speak about it again in the hope that it would disappear and go away.'

I was thirty-seven. I sat down. My head hurt and felt blurry, yet also something was very, very clear.

At the age of nine, something had happened to me in a bedroom that I also stored away deep in my heart and was not willing to feel.

I had chosen to push down and hide this sexual trauma as I was too frightened to talk about it or feel it at the time. So it was easier not to feel. It was easier to resist it.

At nine years old I was burdened with (another) huge block, a samskara. It was too painful to deal with at the time—I didn't have the tools to—and it was easier to create an armour of protection so that my heart couldn't be hurt again.

This trauma that we store and pack away really tight stays as energy. It is like a whirlpool in a pond.

Allow me to introduce Japanese scientist Dr Masaru Emoto. He revolutionised the idea that our thoughts and intentions impact the physical realm, and is one of the most important water researchers the world has known.

Dr Emoto's work was a game changer in helping me understand that, with our thoughts and words, we alter the state of our minds and bodies. His research demonstrates that water exposed to kind words and thoughts of love, gratitude, thankfulness and compassion (with intention and emotion) will form aesthetically pleasing physical molecular formations. On the opposite scale, water exposed to fear, judgement, doubt, hate and anger will develop disconnected, disfigured and unstructured physical molecular formations. He did this through Magnetic Resonance Analysis technology and high-speed photographs.

In our lives, we may have an experience that reminds us of the pain of *that moment* and not know exactly why we contract, feel small or feel shame. This is the block—the samskara—that is being triggered, and is busting to ask you to bring it back up with compassion and feeling, then let it go.

Suddenly, a hell of a lot made sense. The people pleasing, the perfection, the striving to be liked, the feeling of not being enough and the craving of attention could all be connected back to these moments.

Sitting on the sand in a bit of a messy, confused but curious blur, I called my mum and was like, 'Do you remember when I was nine and this happened at ...?'

Suddenly the line went deadly silent.

'Mum?'

In barely a whisper she said, 'Yes, I remember.'

First, this memory came up when I was ready to feel it, experience it, be in the shame and guilt that came with that. And I was able to move through it and let it go. I had held on to it—unconsciously—for long enough.

Second, I have absolutely no blame, anger or resentment for what happened at that time. I choose not to spend the rest of my life beholden to the guilt of something that happened many years ago. I am able to let it go.

For many years I struggled with over-jealous relationships. I had two that were abusive—verbal and physical. I didn't think I was deserving of money (I have realised that too was a story I held on to from early childhood) and I never believed in myself or what I could create.

We are always attracting, never pushing away. Even Ayurveda (Eastern science) says like increases like, which resonates and aligns with the law of attraction. If we are coming from a place of unworthiness, non-acceptance, and low self-worth, more of that comes to us or we are treated in a similar way. If we are confident, self-assured and authentic we will find more abundance and kindness, and genuine love will find us.

I was nine. I was stuck in my head about trying to be liked, pretty, accepted and popular. This wanting energy, craving attention and likes, is an energy field. We can feel when people are desperate or needy and we can feel when they are confident and content.

The same goes for animals, trees, nature and what we do in our environment. We are no different.

Whatever happened, happened. We are all battling our own fight, and we all fuck up somewhere along the way and make mistakes. It's how we grow and learn from them that is important.

These interactions between myself and another were sexually oriented and persuasive, and the by-product that I experienced was shame and guilt. I blamed myself for allowing this to go ahead more than once. At that age, and especially with the belief I already held of myself, I felt accepted as someone's 'special' mate, even though I knew deep in my gut that something was incredibly not right.

Since discovering this for myself, I asked Mum to talk about this experience and why it wasn't discussed when I was younger. For both of us, it was too hard to go there, so the more comfortable option was to not discuss it. How we deal with tough emotions is also down to our conditioning, how we were brought up, our parents and their patterns, their parents and so on. Remember, it just is. It's not wrong or right; we are just doing the best we can with the information we know.

If things were never talked about in your family and that behaviour has been passed down, you are only going to repeat the same blueprint.

It was only quite a few years after the incident that I remember awkwardly bringing up in a shameful, guilty and mumbling voice that something was going on, as I knew right in my gut it didn't 'feel' right.

But almost as quickly as I spoke about it, it was never talked about again. We think if we just forget it ever happened—if we push it away and lock it in a deep, dark box in our hearts— eventually it will fade and disappear, and life will go on.

It was never talked about again until that day nearly twenty years later.

On a side note here, remember how I spoke about the words Nan was still speaking to herself on her last day here on Earth? 'I can't forgive myself. I've been a bad person.' This doesn't just happen. This is a build-up of the stuff we have stashed deep down in our hearts and have been unwilling to feel and let go. If left to fester and grow, these dark emotions of shame, guilt, blame and self-judgement create blockages in our mind, body and heart.

We all go through 'stuff'. All of us move through some sort of traumatic experience. It is up to us as the individual to choose how long we hold on to it. It is also up to us to not keep quiet. The harder we push the stuff down, the more uncomfortable it will be to have it come up later.

It will not just disappear. Speak up and talk about the things that are uncomfortable. Pretending we are fine and 'soldiering on' is, I believe, why Australia has the highest rate of mental health and physiological issues, and suicide. I share some stats on these rates in the next story.

Keep holding on

Nothing is *ever* worth holding on to, so the quicker we enable ourselves to let go of the guilt and shame from our past, the more we can then put that energy of acceptance into practice.

Acknowledge with compassion your wrongdoings—we all have them. Holding on to the should haves, could haves and would haves will keep you stuck in the past, not just in your mind, but in your body. If you are a parent and feel stuck with feelings of blame or guilt for something that has unfolded, this *is not* on you. You have permission to let it go and move forward from here. Be the example that you wish your kids to see.

We will only continue to deepen the wounds of regret if we allow ourselves to hold on to the memory of past transgressions, self-hatred and self-sabotage. It serves us absolutely no benefit at all in the present moment, unless our purpose is to stay in chosen suffering and punishment.

Sport was my vice, then alcohol, online shopping, sex and drugs

By my twenties, I had become used to pushing down feelings and numbing them—replacing them with more striving, more pushing, more perfection, more people pleasing, and of course, more time trying to achieve validation from others to make me feel good.

Nothing ever just disappears. Think of it festering, growing, becoming turbulent. It will come up one day and it will come up at the times you least expect it, unannounced like a thief in the night, and just as confronting, uncomfortable and painful as it was when it was experienced years ago. In my case, I had no idea this old trauma was, in fact, in control of my whole life.

My choices, my thoughts and my actions were governed around this event. I held on to it in my heart, even though I thought I had buried it. This storing of energy—the samskara, the trauma, the impression—started to direct how I felt about myself without me even consciously knowing it was there.

My dialogue with myself became hurtful and unkind, and was on a downward, very well-practised spiral to poor mental, physical and emotional health.

When the things come up

When I discovered this, aged thirty-seven, I realised I had held this inside me for more than twenty years. I had pushed it down so deep that I had forced myself to forget about it and pretend that nothing had ever happened. What I didn't realise, of course, was that the pushing down of these emotions of shame and guilt had an influence on all my words, choices, actions and habits from that age onwards, including my eating disorder, anxiety, cutting, body abuse, financial hardship, spending addiction, drug addiction, addiction to self-sabotage and low self-worth.

I had become used to numbing and running whenever I experienced an emotion I didn't want to feel.

So upon receiving this memory from God, I was ready to dive in. The Universe will only give us what we can handle at the right time, and clearly it was time for me to do the work.

Welcome to a new ride of understanding.

I was so determined to understand, without judging myself, how this had affected my heart, my thoughts, my words and my choices up to this moment.

We always have a choice to become curious, not critical.

Upon this discovery on that game changer of a day at the ocean, Mum and I sat down, almost as sisters with open hearts, and had a discussion around this. It seems that my mum (and I share this with her permission) had also experienced sexual trauma. More than once. This is not uncommon. What was *common* back in the time is that no one talked about it. I'm not just talking about my mother's generation—this stems back for many generations.

It was considered shameful if any of this was discussed, so it was stored.

The way we act when we are reminded of a samskara is dependent on our program—what has been learnt along the way. If we have not allowed ourselves to feel this pain, trauma or suffering when it comes up, we become reactive and relive this in the present moment. When we are triggered in our environment (say someone or something reminds us of how we felt back then), we relive childhood feelings of low self-esteem, the feeling of being being seen and not heard, and the emotions of shame, guilt and blame that we carry with us until we are ready to feel them, heal them and release them.

For many of us in Western society, the message was that it was easier to be busy, pretend we were fine, reach for a drink, overdo work, hit the gym, eat, starve, or shop online. There are still plenty of advertisements and magazines telling us how we can escape from the feelings of pain. I know I'm not the only one who found it easier to skim above the surface of the deep wounds, until I was forced with my body breaking down, to start to slowly face them and heal.

These patterns of conditioning have gone on for many years. Not wrong, not right—they just are. We have to become aware of these patterns to change them and heal them. And that can be uncomfortable.

But we need to chase the uncomfortable in order to create change.

Investigating this further, I studied the book *The Body Keeps the Score* and highly recommend you read Bessel van der Kolk's work to gain an understanding that this was very common not so long ago.

Developing the programmed mind

The Jesuits say, 'Show me the child until they are seven, and I'll show you the man.' Our brains from the age of two to seven are in theta (brainwave) state. This is also known as our hypnotic state, which means we are the learners of everything around us—what we see, hear, and take in from others—and our experiences start to become our truth.

As we get older, it's much harder to access the deep-rooted subconscious mind where our 'programs'—childhood thoughts and beliefs—have been stored. Treatments such as hypnotherapy, meditation, energy work and talking about it to a therapist, friend or healer helps immensely. The more we shove it down, the more physiological issues we will suffer as we get older because this energy cannot get out.

This is why affirmations (with emotion) and setting intentions based on your values are so important before you go to bed, and first thing when you wake up.

I still do the work. I am healing, and always learning the *why* of the actions I choose, the dialogue I speak and the behaviours I adapt. My healing is a journey of curiosity, compassion, and no judgement.

It's also important to note here that none of us are perfect. When I'm knocked out of alignment—through lack of sleep, poor food choices, neglecting movement or being too busy—I make poor choices too and it takes me longer to come back to equilibrium.

The First Noble Truth of Buddhism is that 'all of life is suffering'. It's our ride as to how quickly we can return to presence and make a kind choice for ourselves.

Use your trigger as your teacher

When things show up—as in, something triggers me—I do my best now to investigate why. Why is it that this situation has pushed my buttons? If there is a button there, that is a blockage, a samskara, an invitation to go deep with myself and heal the wound.

I am talking about this because I need to be clear that it was meant to be. It was part of the somewhat messy ride that brought me to where I am now. I choose not to judge it, blame it, hold guilt, shame myself or wish that it were different. All is how it's meant to be and it has unfolded exactly as my life was destined to.

If you or someone you know has been through any sexual abuse or trauma, be gentle and seek help. Talk, share, yield, surrender and get it out somehow. The feelings of shame and guilt can really darken our lives and the more we keep them inside of us, the more we tend to lean into reactivity, blame, judgement and criticism, especially of ourselves. When the things present themselves to be felt and heard, the Universe is giving us permission to heal them and let them go.

You are not alone.

Give yourself permission to learn to feel, and start to heal.

I had to choose to be vulnerable and compassionate with myself. This was something so unfamiliar to me that it took time, many fuck-ups, patience and practice. Each time I caught myself in my story of guilt, shame or blame I started to call it out and recognise the words I was speaking to myself. It was only from this moment that I started to really change my dialogue and understand that I could create a new story.

I used the first three steps of the BE HERE method constantly.

- I see you, body (tension, sore lower back, tight shoulders).
- I feel you, emotion (shame, guilt, blame).
- And it's OK. What does my heart need? ('I choose to be kind to myself today and offer compassion.')

This yielding, surrendering, and acknowledging that I was responsible for all my choices up until this very moment gave me some sort of power. I realised that if I had the will to choose to have an eating disorder, to choose to hang my head over a bowl for more than fifteen years, and to choose to numb with every single thing that I could, then I had the power to will it to be different. That was so fucking powerful and really hit a note with me.

I knew I had the willpower to practise letting it go.

Do not let your past define you

This was part of bringing me to where I am now, and a huge part of my lessons and teachings in life to learn, in time, to stand on my own two feet. To speak up and realise that I'm not my past; I'm the one who is creating the future that is right in front of me now. Not what happened to me, but what is available to me from this moment forward. This choice that is available to all of us can also be a super hard pill to swallow, especially if we have been a victim of our story or label for many years and let it become us.

When it came up, I was ready. I was open to seeing how I could heal my trauma. I got curious about why I was so stuck in familiar patterns of feeling guilty and shameful and blaming others, things and environments for the things happening around me. God only gives you what you can handle at the right time.

The work is always being done. Finding contentment and acceptance is a constant job. I am still working on myself as there are always opportunities to learn and grow.

The shame games

I have taken the viewpoint of shame from the incredible author and shame researcher Brené Brown, which you can read in the 'Shame vs. Guilt' article on her website at brenebrown.com.

Remember, if you catch yourself here in judgement or critical thinking of the self and how you just reacted without thinking, give yourself permission to forgive the thought, action or words, take a deep breath in and choose to be kind to yourself. Do that as often as you need. Remember, watching our language and shifting our self-talk takes time, patience and above all repetition to start to change the hardwiring of the neural pathways of the brain. Keep being gentle with yourself. It's worth the wait.

Journal moment

I ask you to take a minute or two to write down how you may have responded and blamed others or yourself for a situation that happened in your environment, and how it made you feel to project blame rather than sit in feelings of pain, anger, or hurt.

Why do we choose to hang on to these feelings for as long as we do?

If I were doing a seminar, I would open this question up for discussion, and you would be surprised how many of us hang on to these labels because we are terrified of what is underneath. Who is the person that has experienced this, and what is it that we are unwilling to feel? Why do we hang on to it for so long?

Neurologically, we are practising for years sometimes, strengthening the same synaptic connections over and over until they form a very solid cluster of neurons. Once triggered, this cluster almost automatically fires the same reaction day-in day-out as we keep repeating the same words, choices and behaviours.

Again, for shit to change we need to change our shit. We need to come back to the BE HERE method, which allows us to step into presence, pause, and choose again.

But, but, but

Interestingly (and also cringeworthy and confronting), from my research I believe we hold on to our limiting beliefs and dialogue. It keeps us in a pattern of excuses. I certainly spent much time in one.

Oh, this happened to me when I was little. Therefore I ...

I'll never be able to do that because I failed at it when I was ...

My body can't do that as I had this injury years ago and I don't want it to happen again.

People will judge me if I speak my truth and be authentic. Others may not like me. It's easier to be the person everyone knows me to be.

I feel safe. I know this story well and I don't know who I am underneath this belief. What if it disrupts my partner or my family, or people disown me?

What if you were able to give yourself permission to let go of the old belief pattern? I guarantee you it's definitely not true anymore.

Spend some time on how good this feels

It will only be true if you choose it to be and continue to give it your energy and attention.

Try this affirmation and see how it feels: 'I am the only one who is able to change my story. I am worthy of feeling free, content, and accepting of myself just as I am.'

We all go through the shit. We all have felt shame, guilt and blame.

Newsflash: you are not alone.

Nope, not at all. I have done many workshops and plan to do many more. Your story is relevant and needs to be honoured. Every single one of us has suffered guilt, shame and blame.

The duration that we choose to hold on to it is completely up to us.

Isn't that amazing to hear?

'But,' I hear you say, 'I just can't stop the thoughts.'

'I keep reverting to old ways of thinking and doing.'

'I'm too old to change and I don't know how.'

'I don't know who I am anymore or my purpose.'

Remember, with neuroplasticity we are constantly replacing our cells until we die.

> When you change the way you look at things,
> the things you look at change.
> — Wayne Dyer

Once we stop giving this cluster of neurons—let's say a collection of beliefs of the 'not enough' story—our energy, we start to fire and wire new neurons that stem from positive affirmations and beliefs such as *I am deserving of love and compassion, I am worthy, I am abundant* and *I am grateful to get to have today—thank you.* We build a slow but sure connection of good-feeling thoughts that start to strengthen a new cluster while the other starts to lose its power. This is all about repetition.

The same goes for how you talk to yourself in the mirror. If the first thing you say to yourself is 'I wish I were ...' or 'I wish I looked like ...' or you grimace at yourself and affirm the 'not enough' dialogue ... then you are headed for more struggle. We need to catch it in the moment and shift it by looking ourselves in the eye and telling our beautiful self just how incredible and amazing we are. Trust me. The body that is staring back at you is there anyway. You may as well get freaking pumped about it and boost yourself up rather than shoot yourself down.

Try it now. Go find a mirror. Look into your eyes. Say out loud: 'I am incredible, beautiful and deserving. Today I honour you, respect you and love you. You are amazing.' Then go slay.

Flip the script

Let's take our shame, guilt, blame and judgement and turn it into our teacher.

OK. So are you constantly feeling resentful, judgemental and comparing, or are you grounded in gratitude?

This should spark a question within yourself. If your thoughts are more skewed towards judgement, comparison and poor self-talk, then it's a beautiful message to be heard here to tune back into your own self-care, self-acceptance, and kindness for yourself before others.

In the next story we will see how shame, guilt, blame, anger and suppressed emotions get held in the body.

'But this is all I know how to feel,' I hear you say.

I get that completely, and I hear you. It's OK. In fact, I had a conversation with a gorgeous friend who shared a beautiful, empowering message to all women to accept themselves as they are. It was about how we, as humans, are so conditioned to put ourselves down automatically. Constantly in a state of perfection, saying sorry for ourselves, people pleasing or not speaking up for fear of being judged by others. So we stay small.

Conditioning

Truth bomb: you are the product of your thoughts, actions, choices and words right up to this very moment.

How does that feel? Take a moment to digest this. It might be getting a somewhat reactive 'fuck you' at the moment and that's OK.

I just ask you to indulge me here for a bit.

I used to get, and still do to this day, 'It's easy for you to say ... look at you. You're fit, healthy, strong ... what do you know about feeling unworthy?'

Sometimes we can assume that someone's physical appearance suggests they have not been through any difficult times or trauma. Most times, when we are triggered by others and reactive, there is something inside of us that has not been healed yet.

Disordered eating can go either way. When I was unwell, people would still comment on me being 'skinny' or the say, 'Why won't you just eat?'

On a side note—never ever comment on the body of someone who is struggling. Especially in the case of an eating disorder. That person will take that as ammo and use that drive of looking sick to lose more weight. (Yes, the mind of an eating disorder sufferer is messy, hence why it is so important to understand that Ana or Mia can be a dangerous second person.)

Body shaming of any kind is unnecessary and judgemental. It says more about the person who is judging than the one being judged.

I am, however, so proud of myself for getting to where I am physically, spiritually and mentally. I never ever thought being in this state was possible, and as mentioned, if I can feel a love that is so powerful and full of acceptance for myself, then there is no doubt you can too.

It starts with a belief that you can adapt right now! That you always have been and always will be worthy. And that belief must be something you feel energetically.

I used to be so caught up in how I felt I needed to act or what I needed to do, for society and for others, to be accepted in a world that was based purely on the opinion of others. My conditioning was so strong I had no idea what it was to be like to be me.

Whatever is unfolding in front of us is going to happen anyway. It is up to us how we choose to react or respond. (More on this later.)

If our thoughts and words have the power to change the crystallisation of water to a state of distortion and unease (sickness), is it possible that our thoughts and words are able to find equanimity, harmony and balance with the body (wellness)?

Take a moment to indulge your younger self and remember what was unfolding in front of you.

A few things come to my mind. Seeing *Aerobics Oz Style* on TV and tiny waists. The Lite n' Easy or Weight Watchers ads always talking about calories and being slim. Billboards, posters and commercials showing ridiculously thin models.

The 'waif' body type and the 'heroin chic' look became popular.

In 1995, Ivana Trump told *The New York Times*: 'If I am working I'd rather have the lean and hungry feel.'

Diet culture started to really take flight and it seemed everyone was on a diet.

From my experience and through online coaching, it seems that many people still are.

I would see *Cosmo*, *Girlfriend*, *Dolly* and *New Idea* mags around the house and at my mates' places. And the rise of *Baywatch*, Pammy and the 'perfect' bikini body.

I surveyed a group of women aged thirty to forty-five on what they remember—their responses were:

1. 'My parents and how they were told to act or look.'
2. Pinching of the skin and belly through puberty. I remember my mother pinching my hips and belly when I was about eleven or twelve. Puberty was making changes to my body, but I was warned, 'Watch that— you're getting a little pudgy.' So these days, loving my body is a big fuck you to that bullshit.
3. 'Ford Pills, laxatives, workout videos, Jane Fonda, cabbage soup diet, rise of lite products (milk, cheese), leotards with belts, *Cleo* and *Dolly* magazines. Even movies such as *Dirty Dancing* and *Flashdance*, bikini body with the rise of surfing, baggy clothes to hide your body.'
4. 'Comments made from family (male members): "Watch what you're eating—all that going back for seconds will go to your hips." In high school, bulimia was common, but it was known as being "cool" to throw up after dinner. Also, for me, what stands out growing up is Barbie (no one looks like that), and the so-called perfect skin, hair and body. I remember as a kid wanting to look like her.'

5. 'Weight was always on the forefront of both [the minds of] my mother and grandmother and they weighed themselves daily. My favourite saying from my grandmother was "You can never be too rich or too thin." They never dieted per se, but always watched the scales. My first real negative body issues began in Years 6–9 where I was tall and gangly [and had] no boobs … as the *Baywatch* bodies were a thing, I planned for a boob job as soon as I was eighteen. I never wanted to be "waify" but always wanted a skinnier stomach as I always had a "jelly belly". Lastly, I was a "fat shamer" when I was younger, mainly because I worked so hard on how I looked and always said (in my head) *If only they tried harder, ate less,* etc. … Now I feel women should wear whatever makes them feel proud. Healthy is what we all should be.'

All of these beliefs stem from the images, media, magazines, social media, toys and TV programs that were conditioned into us as kids. Again, it is always a choice as to how we see these things, and what influences us when we are growing up, such as how our parents, carers or teachers responded with their own thoughts, words and actions.

My question here is: do these things ring true for you still? Do we really need to keep firing and wiring the same old story that does nothing for us?

What does this have to do with shame, guilt and blame? If we are still battling with these emotions that have been stored deep down, we are going to continually be affected by what we see around us, as we are not content in our bodies as we are. We will always be looking for something to change, adapt or perfect so we can look 'somewhat similar' to what we are seeing in the mainstream.

Do you really think this will be possible? Do you believe it starts with you or is it too hard to change?

In my courses I ask people the question straight up. 'Do you *believe* you can change?' Usually the answer is a weak 'yes' or a 'not really', but by the end we have been able to shift our energy and that question is then answered with a big EFF YES!

If we have been conditioned for generations on end to look a certain way, fit a certain body type, have a smaller waist or keep our hips to a certain size, yes it's damn hard. But remember, what we practise gets stronger, so watching our language now will start to make changes for future generations and how they will see themselves and their bodies. It provides the tools to share this view of compassion and love with others.

Advertising has shaped our world

A 2015 Harvard T.H. Chan School of Public Health article on 'Advertising's Toxic Effect on Eating and Body Image' states: 'People often claim to ignore advertisements, but the messages are getting through on a subconscious level.' The author goes on to deconstruct the messages in food and body-image advertisements and describe how they create a toxic cultural environment that harms our relationship with what we eat.

The article states that, in 2015, the average American encountered three thousand advertisements every day and spent a total of two years watching commercials and advertising in their lifetime. This number would now be increased incredibly with the rise of social media. 'At the centre of many of these ads is an image of idealised female beauty,' the article states. 'Models are tall, slim, and light-skinned, and digitally altered to ever-more unrealistic proportions.' (I will dive into the modern version of this very shortly with Snapchat and selfie dysmorphia.)

Women and girls, and now men, are comparing themselves to these images every day, 'and failure to live up to them is inevitable because they are based on a flawlessness that does not exist,' ad critic Jean Kilbourne told the Harvard T.H. Chan School of Public Health. The article goes on to say:

> The American ideal of beauty has become so pervasive that 50% of three- to six-year-old girls worry about their weight. And on the island of Fiji, the arrival of television heralded a boom in dieting among women and girls who before hadn't realised there was something wrong with them.

They hadn't realised there was something wrong with them. Read that again.

A STORY ON ITS OWN

THE SELFIE ADDICTION

Selfie and snapchat dysmorphia

Behind the cat videos, the addictive dances and the fitness hacks, there is a darker side to TikTok than most of us know. I have spent the past three years researching this app alongside Instagram and the harmful, dangerous and neurally rewarding dopamine hits it is giving young minds.

Algorithms fuel more of what we are searching. So, of course, if we are struggling with disordered eating and mental health, what we are searching for may not be healthy. In fact, it's likely to be topics that help us stay stuck and unwell. This repetition of seeing the same becomes what we know and is how we develop a sense of not feeling enough as we are.

It took me less than thirty seconds to find harmful content on TikTok, and a few hours for the algorithm to dominate my feed with the content that was showing how to lose weight and get a thigh gap, or how to stay under forty-five kilos (yes, this is a thing), vomit silently and not eat for three days.

We can go on these apps with the right intentions, but I have worked with adults and children who have found that by searching things like 'fitness', 'diet', 'calorie counting' and 'fit trends', they have easily been directed through the algorithm to content that is promoting disordered eating, unhealthy body image and an ideal of how we 'should' look.

In short, there are videos that are teaching people how to have an eating disorder.

This is absolutely NOT OK.

During my research, I was bombarded with many influencers telling me how to stay under five-hundred calories a day, how to pretend that I had eaten a meal, and what to do if I had overeaten.

More children, with the biggest rise by teenage girls aged 12 to 17, used hospital mental health services after the first lockdown than reported in the past five years. This is why I am so determined to share this information. Not one of us, or our kids, deserves to feel this way about themselves.

Alarmingly, as I am writing this, the content mentioned does not breach TikTok's guidelines. On my Instagram page, and during live presentations, I speak openly about how some of these accounts can be so dangerous.

Certain words are banned. However, there are hashtags that can be spelt differently with extra letters or manipulated to still carry the same heartbreaking content. It's just about being aware.

Anything in excess becomes harmful

TikTok is not bad. It is how we use it that can be damaging. Just like food. If we eat too much we become unwell.

Welcome to the world we are in today. The ultimate, I believe, in not feeling enough as you are.

Here is the rise of unworthiness, low self-worth and unacceptance of who we are on a whole new level.

This is something to be super aware of if you are the parent of a teen, no matter their gender, or maybe it's something you have become addicted to yourself. Just like anorexia, bigorexia is a thing: guys not feeling big enough to post pics of themselves for fear of judgement or trolls. It's not just eating disorders—kids, of any gender, are now becoming addicted to their modified and filtered self. This is where it becomes harmful.

The 2021 article 'An ode to plastic surgeons on world plastic surgery day' published by the *Logical Indian* states:

> [The] phenomenon of people requesting procedures to resemble their digital image has been referred to as "Snapchat dysmorphia". The term was coined by cosmetic doctor Tijion Esho, founder of the Esho clinics in London and Newcastle.

Anti-wrinkle injection procedures (including Botox, fillers and laser skin treatments) are on the rise. I can't help but think if they're having cosmetic procedures now, will they then seek to continue them for a lifetime?

Addicted to a modified version of ourselves

These days, people around the world are seeking surgery that matches their Instagram- or Snapchat-filtered selfies, such as the anime eye, airbrushed skin, high cheekbones, sculpted eyebrows, narrowed chins, cute nose and plumped lips. It's not just our photos either; videos are not immune to a good old edit on an Instagram feed. If you think this is startling, hold on to your seat: body parts can be edited removing belly rolls, hip dips, and cellulite. Add in a sprinkle of trimmed waists (including removing ribs), butt lifts, sixpacks (not the beer kind), toned shoulders, extra muscles, thicker quads, and longer legs and we have what you may call the recipe for the perfect selfie.

If you are not shaking in your boots, you should be. Please know my sharing of this information is to inform, not avoid, the very real unfolding of a situation that will affect our teens and kids, and then their own. When we know, we can do something about it.

What can we do? Check in on our own feeds, posts and use of filters and apps. Without judgement, and without criticism, consider how you are showing up as a parent or carer, and what your kinds are leaning from your own actions, behaviours and dialogue.

The dark side

Now you can understand why I have been a bit of a hermit the last few years with this research. It's dark, but my dharma is to bring this to light and redirect our world back to self-love. My research has taken me to the darker side of these apps, which is the backbone of my second book, *The Perfection Pandemic*. There are now Chinese apps that evaluate your face and give it a score from one to one hundred based on how beautiful and attractive you are.

You might want to pick your jaw up off the floor.

Wait for it … Once you have your score, your face is then broken down piece by piece and you are told what is wrong with it and what you need to do to 'fix it'. And it gets better … many plastic surgeons in the country have collaborated with the app and offer their services to teen and adult users so they can book asap to get the 'perfect' face. They offer payment plans and all so that we can move towards a perfect society: so we can now look like our Instagram and TikTok feeds.

Insert forehead slap here.

Don't worry; I've got you. I'm not here to play small. My mission is to have apps like this banned across the world. Remember, I am a woman on a mission to change the world. To me, this is the guts of Watch YA Language: if we can't even be honest and authentic with ourselves, then how do we expect our dialogue to serve us (and others)?

As I tweak the final edits of this book, I am now in the process of running workshops for all schools and their parents/carers based on the power of showing up. Every second there are more and more teens (and adults) who are struggling to post real content because we feel so conditioned now to be perfect and flawless and fit what are unrealistic and unattainable expectations.

My concern lies with those who are in a world of unawareness. Maybe it's happening repetitively with our carers, our siblings, our friends or our parents. If we are using them, this is just a gentle nudge to be aware. What is the message behind using? Why do we feel the need, and what is the underlying teaching that this imparts.

Images and videos that are modified using apps promote the drive towards perfection and people pleasing, and from here is only a downhill spiral of poor mental, physical and emotional health.

Everything, and I mean everything, can be modified using these apps.

We are being taught that we need to be an edited, modified or beautified version of ourselves to be popular, liked and enough.

Where does the line stop?

It must stop with us. Choosing to be authentic, putting the first photo up without an edit, being OK with an imperfect angle and embracing our imperfections is how (I believe) we teach our little ones to do that too. We can only show not tell.

This is most accurately described as conditioning. Everywhere we look we are taught to believe we are not enough as we are. We are too thick, too flabby, not tall enough, not pretty enough. Our skin is too flawed, our waist too boxy, our jaw not sharp enough, our eyes not big enough, our bellies not taut enough and our shoulders not toned enough.

This is where your practice of presence comes in. How long do we choose to allow ourselves to be affected by this, and can we start to tell ourselves a new story? That is up to you. Your choice of backing your authenticity—being totally OK with who you are without the need for more—will share a very powerful message to those around you that they can also be OK with their body, and not feel the need to alter or change it to fit in with society.

I invite you to stop for one moment and read that last paragraph again.

Do we realise just how ridiculous all of this comparing, judging and criticising really is? Come on. But we still do it, right? Why? It's due to the many years we have been conditioned to think we are not enough as we are. Thanks, advertising.

Remember, if you believed these things about yourself—about not feeling enough in some sort of way—through your will, then you have the will to change it.

Give.

Yourself.

Time.

A dangerous addiction to perfection

Let me go a little further. The disturbing end point for Snapchat and selfie dysmorphia is suicide. Plastic surgeons are seeing a huge surge in procedures, and statistically the number is rising every day on suicides linked to selfie dysmorphia. These people have developed such an addiction to their edited self that they cannot go outside for fear of looking different.

A desire for approval, a longing for acceptance, an addiction for validation that is driving our society away from connection … This addiction to the perfect selfie (or body) creates a constant firing and wiring of neurons that, with practice and repetition, rewires our brain to believe we are unworthy and unlovable as we are.

What a ridiculous joke, right? But it is what it is and it is here to stay, for now. So we must ask ourselves, how do we go about our own social media? Do we speak out loud when we post a photo that we think is awful or frumpy? Do we speak words of unkindness to ourselves when we look in the mirror or see an image someone else has posted? Those words do not go unnoticed. You hear them and reaffirm the old limiting belief in your mind, and possibly, your little ones may also be taking this (and your energy) on board.

What your social media says about you

This is where I dive a little deeper into something that is fascinating, terrifying and in all of our faces whether we like it or not. I have not been exempt from what we are about to discuss. It is awareness and practice that helps bring us back to our authenticity and own it.

I am talking about the need to please others or seek validation through presenting an image that is acceptable in society.

Why is it that we feel the need to present an image to the world that is different to how we are actually feeling?

Because we are so used to avoiding the not-so-glamorous truth, we then allow ourselves other little lies and stories that paint a picture of a truly different life than what we are actually living.

How long can we continue this lie? Well, the answer is up to you.

All that has been learnt can be unlearnt.

For years I used to post on my accounts a picture-perfect Meg who looked like she had her shit together. Big smiles, edited images, good angles, and captions that were loaded with BS and the complete opposite of how I was feeling at the time.

Oh, and sometimes this took hours, hundreds of photos, and a constant judging of my photos not being worthy ... no kidding.

I posted to get likes, to confirm that I was worthy of acceptance from others, for the validation that I was enough.

I used to post about my body a lot and say:

'Still not quite there yet, but on my way.'
'It's not perfect, but I'm working on it.'
'Gaining muscles slowly, but a long way off.'

In other words, I was reaching out for comments from others such as:

'Hot.'
'Stunning.'
'You're so pretty.'
'Gun.'
'Cute.'
'Gorgeous.'
'Body!'

Or, ones like this that egged me to do it more: 'What do you mean? You look AMAZING in that pic!'

Over time, this becomes an addiction not dissimilar to cocaine or sugar. It raises dopamine levels in our brains to the extent that we become addicted to our phones, the notification buzz when we get a new like or comment, and the constant checking to see if we have reached more likes than the last photo.

This addiction becomes a practice and it creates our environment. More on this in the final story.

What's the story behind the image

For every image we edit or change, there is a scar that we need to heal.

Let's get out from under the filters, the skin-perfecting tools, the adjusting of our images, the smoothing of our skin and the tucking in of our waists, our bellies and our thighs. Hands up if you have ever modified a photo. I have definitely used filters before (and I still use them every now and then when I'm looking for a fun, playful theme), however I believe hands down that body- and face-editing apps are bullshit. There is no way that any good can come from you editing bumps out of your tummy and thighs just because social media says they are not OK.

This, in my eyes, needs to be banned. I will not stop until I have done all I can to have these stopped. The research is clear and it's heartbreaking. I truly believe it is affecting our mental health rates across the world.

There is a reason underneath this that all of us are not so proud of, in most circumstances. It's because we are feeling not enough as we are, and we are trying to fit the bill of how we think we should look to fit in with society's expectations and conditioning of the 'perfect image'.

We are trying to fit into an environment that we have created due to conditioning and the social media expectations around us.

It's subtle, but it's also something that's difficult to stop when we start it.

I am not saying that using filters, editing tools and adjustments are a bad thing. But when they are used to 'perfect' an image, or change your body shape or face to fit in with a standard in your head that you think you need to adhere to, it is not OK.

Perfection is slowly killing us. It's making us tired, stressed, agitated, annoyed, overwhelmed, exhausted and judgemental—constantly having us search for more, more and more! If we are always searching, we will always be looking. It's time for you now to give up that chase and let perfection go. It's time now to do you.

This constant practice of modifying our images, tucking in our bellies, slimming our waists, smoothing our skin, making ourselves taller, lengthening our limbs, accentuating our cheekbones, perfecting our noses, whitening and brightening our eyes, making our eyes wider, smoothing out our wrinkles, adjusting our jaw and changing our whole fucking bodies is an addiction and a practice that will never provide you with happiness; it will just increase the limiting belief of feeling not enough.

And we *know* this is just an old story.

The truth behind the scenes

I downloaded TikTok with curiosity, but deep down I was terrified of what I knew I would find.

There are three big reasons why I didn't want to enter the TikTok world:

1. Addiction
2. Another app to post to or get caught scrolling in
3. The dark side of it that I knew I would see

I have recently created an account on there under @meg_watchyalanguage so that I can share real content in regards to body image, eating disorders and mental health. There are also many others sharing some really great content to combat what you see.

In my YouTube research on body image, and Snapchat/selfie dysmorphia and eating disorders, one particular user caught my attention, and not in a good way. Without mentioning her name, she holds one of the biggest YouTube accounts in the world and, alongside her mother, glorifies having an eating disorder.

Eating disorders, mental health and suicide numbers have increased substantially since the introduction of these apps, YouTube accounts and websites in support of what's called 'pro-ED'. This was telling me it was now time to investigate the side of this app that was fuelling the fire of the young users frequenting it.

Hashtags from hell

The hashtag #skinny has been banned from TikTok, but I was able to type in #skiny, #skinnny and many similar words to produce just the content I was searching for. I also dived into #diet, #dietculture, #caloriecounting, #weightloss, #advice, #bdd, #bodydysmorphia and #ed as well as #edrecovery, #recovery and #skinbones, and it wasn't the content so much that scared the shit outta me; it was all the comments of self-regret, self-sabotage, disbelief and judgement that were to follow under the posts, which showed just how many of us struggle with our self-image and -esteem.

Be reminded that although we sometimes cannot change what goes on or control our environment, we can choose to see it differently and not let it control us.

We can choose to put the work into ourselves.

I spent more than three years diving into these trends, hashtags and comments, and of course the YouTube accounts that follow. I had never realised just how big the problem is that we are facing today when it comes to comparison, perfection and the need for more.

Apps, including any social media, are a good distraction for when we feel emotions we don't want to sit with. So when young adults feel fear, anxiety, worry or depression, it's easy to scroll, numb and get lost in a world that is far away from their feelings.

I mentioned a few pages back those terrifying stats. When we have constant access to a popular social media app that is programmed to ding, beep and notify us when we have new likes, comments and shares, we can become so addicted to the chase for validation that feeling our feelings is easily replaced by numbing (scrolling).

This is where we become stuck in our environment and where we continually put our energy and attention. And that will only grow.

Think about this for a moment. When we feel emotions we don't want to feel, it's easy to numb with online shopping, alcohol, exercise, or drugs.

For kids, they have their phones and watches. So the repetitive action of picking up their device and scrolling through their chosen feed is a recipe for more thoughts and words of unworthiness, self-doubt and low self-esteem.

This is a real thing and deserves a book on its own, but for now, hopefully I can leave you with the thought of, *Yes, this is affecting myself and my kids/the young people in my life, and maybe there is something I can do to show up a little more for myself.*

Get in touch on my website to book these talks for your region or school. Check out watchyalanguage.com/schools.

Journal moment

I know this is a huge topic, but my heart would not allow it to go unnoticed. I want you to write down an affirmation you can say to yourself when you post your next photo. Can you post it to be proud of you, not for the number of likes and comments or validation from others?

From someone who has been there

For someone who has an eating disorder, the words *You look so sick, Why can't you just eat? I'm worried for you* and the rest are bait like a bone to a dog.

Keep going, eat less and stay unhealthy … What I am doing is working.

Many users dropping pro-ED content leave the comment section open on all channels. In my opinion (and experience), this is the user's way of validating the eating disorder.

Again, it's a tick in the box that the eating disorder is doing its job and 'sick' is exactly how they want to look.

I share this content here because it's plastered online for all to see. It's not edited, it's not private, and it's certainly not what should be on the feeds of young kids who are in any body image battle.

I feel only compassion for these influencers. I do truly hope they find a way out of their battle, use their struggles as a light for others, and help their millions of subscribers to regain health.

That would be a powerful message and it is exactly what we are here to do in the world. We are often given tough times so that we can do the work, learn what we need to from the trauma or pain, and then share our experience with others who are going through a similar journey.

THE INNER WORK

You are the creator of your environment

Yes I keep banging on about this, I know, but being the creator of your environment really is the key to watching your own language.

Your words.

Your thoughts.

Your actions.

Your posts.

Your energy dictates the message you share with others. The law of attraction has been around long enough for us all to understand that what we create, we get more of.

If we are getting around with a sense of unworthiness and low self-esteem, then that message will transfer to all around us. People will pick up on your energy and start to mirror the same.

Mirror neurons

Others are mirrors reflecting ourselves back to us.

If we feel we are being judged, then we are judging others. If we feel someone is jealous of us, then we are feeling jealous of them. If we feel someone is excluding us, then we may be unconsciously excluding them.

They will be one of your biggest teachers.

Think about a time when you were with a work colleague. They are feeling off, having a shitty day and have complained for the twentieth time about the stale cookies in the lunch room. You feel tired, drained, exhausted and a little anxious, just like them. You do your best to stay present but are constantly pulled down by the energy of your friend and can't wait for the lunch date to be over.

Flip the situation. You meet up with your best mate who is vibing from her recent yoga class. The convo is fresh, conscious and alive and you feel energised, uplifted and vibrant from her energy. You walk away feeling on top of the world and ready to inspire the next person who crosses your path.

These mirror neurons develop before we are one year old. One of the major discoveries of mirror neurons occurred in the 1990s when a group of neurophysiologists placed electrodes in the ventral premotor cortex of a macaque monkey. This was to study neurons specifically for the control of the hands and mouth. In the study, they recorded electrical signals from the monkey's brain while the monkey was allowed to reach for pieces of food. This enabled the researchers to measure the neuronal response to certain movements.

What they found, accidentally, was that some of the neurons

they recorded would respond when the monkey *saw* a person pick up a piece of food as well as when the monkey itself picked up the food.

Just by watching, the monkey was able to mirror the action of picking up the food as if it were doing it itself.

Based on this study and many more, it is fair to say that mirror neurons allow us to experience another's emotions. These brain cells fire when you do something and *when you watch someone else do the same thing.* They allow us to mimic what others are doing. It is believed these neurons may be responsible for empathy—the experience of understanding or 'feeling' others' intentions or states of mind.

For me, this also ties in with our intuition, a sense of picking up on another's energy.

Notice the comments on your Facebook feed when they are judgemental, resentful and angry.

We can feel and notice when someone dangerous walks into a room. We experience gushy warmth when someone is completely open and vulnerable with us, offering permission to give back the same.

So hopefully you may understand that what we put out, we get back. The addiction is real with TikTok and Instagram. You can constantly scroll through your feed with endless entertainment and algorithms that are tailored to your liking—good or bad.

Ditch the diet culture

Never cook, eat or serve food in an energy of anger, judgement, self-sabotage or frustration. That energy will only go into the food and have a negative effect on your body and mind.

To end on a higher and more uplifting note: it is a choice as to how we spend our energy and attention. If you are needing inspiration from people who share some downright goodness on health, movement and our bodies, there are some incredible accounts out there. Please check the Resources section at the back of the book.

Again, I could write a whole book on how to change our relationship with food as I believe this is a game changer for lifting our self-worth, acceptance and love for ourselves.

Unfortunately we are all in a world that is telling us to diet, cut carbs, go keto, fast, eat this and eliminate that, and it's so damn confusing. If you are on a diet right this second, I encourage you to do what you can and use the resources and practitioners I have provided (at the back of the book) to start to get to know and listen to your body. You will never diet again once you learn what it is that our bodies need.

Of course, this is just my own research and study with my own body, from someone who was on a diet or plan for more than thirty years. I have been intermittently fasting now for nearly six years and it serves me well. I move a lot and I adjust my energy intake depending on what I do that day. What I do is different to what you need. Just because this is what I do to maintain equilibrium, this does not mean that it may work for you. Your body will tell you what you need.

I never think about calories, macros or last night's meal. It's a waste of time. I put all my energy and attention into loving the food that I am able to enjoy and grow from; I let it nurture my body. And if I do, it means I'm out of alignment—what a great lesson! And that's when I return to the BE HERE method. It's about consistently doing the work.

Presence, awareness and knowledge are our key to understanding what feels good for us.

It's not just food, but who we follow on our feeds, the information we choose to digest from TV or magazines, our work environment and potential gossip or pedestalling. There are many ways we can be in a negative energy state when we are on autopilot.

Ayurveda—the science of life

Now that you have spent the last five minutes trying to pronounce this word, I'll break it down for you: *eye-err-veyda*.

And what the hell does that mean? The balancing of the body and mind.

I want to share with you what has helped me understand just how important it is to communicate with and listen to the body and to understand where we are sitting in our nervous system. If reoccurring illnesses, inflammation or blockages continue to appear in your body year upon year, then I urge you to dive into researching and becoming curious about the ancient science of life, Ayurveda.

Below are some basic guidelines I do my best to live by from the ancient science of Ayurvedic medicine:

1. Scrape tongue after waking up to reduce toxins
2. Drink a glass of warm filtered lemon water
3. Move or meditate
4. ONLY eat when you are hungry and eat to balance your energy
5. Stop when you are full
6. *Always* sit down to eat a meal and try to chew your food ten to twenty times so digestion has time to register fullness
7. Eat non-processed foods that have come from a kind and loving environment and cook your food with love

8. Eat with gratitude and appreciation (I believe this is the most important one)
9. Avoid eating late so that you can digest your food before sleep
10. Go to bed feeling slightly hungry

Balancing the wheels of our vehicle

In my online courses, I share the very basics of Ayurveda that I have dived into and learned from my own teachers. This truly has been a game changer for me in learning to listen to my body from the inside out and I hope that it motivates you to investigate this amazing science further.

For the purposes of this book and gaining a basic understanding, I will share the concepts that helped me gain the right amount of knowledge to dive in and do the work.

Ayurveda has two main concepts:

1. The body and mind are connected
2. Nothing has more power to heal the body than the mind

Within these concepts, this ancient science inherently provides the information that deep down, we know within our bodies. That there is the possibility that we are able to heal ourselves.

I will share with you two models of balance. One in the physical, one in the energetic realm of living a fulfilled, healthy and vibrant life. This is shared from my own understanding and research of principles dated back to nearly five thousand years.

The wheels are falling off

Recently, as I was on my way to teach a sunrise movement

class, I noticed something felt a bit odd. But, since I had had a huge week (or ten), I was running late, a little flustered and not particularly paying attention. If I'm honest, I was trying to nut out the 6.00 am class in my head ten minutes before the session.

It had been a hectic month or two. As I drove, my awareness shifted from lizard crawls, squat transitions and handstands to the *clunk, clunk, clunk* of my car not travelling so smoothly ... but even at this point did I not stop. No, I was running late and I completely dismissed the noise. Four streets, four corners and one sad deflated tyre later, I was pulled up on the side of the road and going nowhere fast. I had to ask for help.

Too often we are on the doing train of striving, overwhelm and busyness and we are unable to notice the wheels falling off one by one. Our bodies start to tell us the moment we are shifting out of balance. But we need to be quiet enough to be able to hear.

These concepts stemming from the ancient teachings of Ayurveda helped me start to listen to my body, to recognise without judging that something was up and needed my immediate attention, rather than keep driving down the road, thinking something may be wrong but ignoring the deep sense of knowing that my tyre is about to blow.

The four components of balance

These four aspects of the body are up to us to maintain and be aware of on a consistent basis. This comes from presence, attentiveness and self-care.

1: The doshas—energies

Doshas are energies present in the body and mind. They also present in our environment. These energies are made up of the five elements: ether, air, fire, water and earth.

Nature is us and we are nature. If we experience too much or too little of something, we start to tip out of equilibrium and things start to topple downhill. On an exceptionally basic level, too much air (Vata) and we are too fast, have trouble concentrating and sleeping, are late and unreliable, and feel dry, unstable and unsettled. Too much Pitta (fire) and we are hot-headed, aggressive, agitated and fired up. And lastly, too much Kapha (earth) and we feel sluggish, shut down, slow, stagnant and unmotivated.

There is so much more to the study of these energies, but that is not for this book. For now, I would love to share the very basics that have helped me understand how to stay regulated and well.

When these energies, the doshas, are out of balance—as in tipping too far into one of them—we will land in a stress state: a place of unease, tension and imbalance. We dive into this a lot more in my Free Your Flow online course.

2: Dhatus—tissues
When we are unable to be in balance, we start to create imbalance in the physical body. Our *dhatus* (tissues) start to struggle to repair. They say that 'the issues are in the tissues' and when our repair state is in disarray, we are on a journey to dis-ease. This involves our epithelial, connective, muscle and nervous tissues that are essential for our health.

3: Agni—digestive fire
The third wheel of balance is our digestive fire, our *agni*. If we are constantly in overdrive, in our sympathetic state (fight-or-flight) or on the busy train, we are essentially putting out our fire. Energy is directed to the heart and lungs and to our muscles

to run from the so-called threat of losing our keys, being late for work, being cut off on the way to work ... you get the idea. We are stressed out over every little thing that comes our way and we stay in a heighted state of overdrive. We get burnt out, so to speak, and as mentioned earlier, we lose our spark.

When our agni 'burns out', things essentially get stuck; nothing moves. This leads us to the fourth pillar of balance...

4: Malas—waste

If we are constantly living in a heightened state of stress, we will have issues peeing and pooping. They say that the average human living in the Western world can be in this state up to one hundred and fifty times per day. That is going to cause havoc for our bodies in clearing out toxicity and waste products. We will get a build-up, which essentially is the early onset of sickness, inflammation and dis-ease

Balancing the mind, body and spirit

On an emotional/mental level, I have found these four pillars are what I come back to often to make sure I am looking after my mental, spiritual and emotional health.

1: Dharma (purpose)

Dharma is what drives our soul forward. It is our cargo, as mentioned earlier, to serve and give back to others. We do not have to go looking for our dharma; it's already within us. We just need to remove the layers and listen.

Too often we are running on empty and operating on autopilot, which is why listening to our intuition can be so hard, especially if we are always living in the past and the future (as I did for many years).

2: Artha (material wealth)

What we have is not us. What we own is not ours. What we live in (our body) is not who we are. It is important to enjoy these things but not attach to them. When we attach to a car, a job, a person, a body or what we own, we can create unnecessary suffering by holding on.

I hear all the time in my coaching, 'If only I could get back to the body I had ten years ago' or 'I'll be happy when I lose that last five kilos.'

No. No, you won't.

Happiness is right here within us, not what we own. Gain wealth with a humble and accepting mindset and utilise with gratitude the universal abundance that is available for all of us: it's everywhere, but use it with the right intention and to serve.

3: Moksha (enlightenment)

I feel *moksha* ties in so well with *artha*. This is it. Right here and now, we have all we need, and I believe enlightenment is available to us in any moment. This is freedom from the body and mind and not basing our happiness on what we have, own or look like. Our true consciousness lies beyond these things.

The true practice of non-attachment can be so hard in the world we live in and is something I continually do my best to practise each day. As someone who was so connected to how I looked on a physical level, I do feel this is achievable with practice and it feels so freeing.

4: Kama (sensory pleasure)

Kama reminds me of doing our best to stay neutral, similar to what we have discussed with the samskaras. To not get overly excited when we hit the highs, and to also not supress or push down the low moments. To experience them all fully without creating a story.

If you were to sit in on a musician playing piano in a dark, intimate bar, you would be clinging on to every note. The highs are just as much a part of the music as the low notes: you would not walk out as soon as they played the deeper notes. The same goes for our experiences. They are all experiences: we get to have them, some are amazing, some are challenging. If we overindulge in the pleasures, we leave ourselves open for behavioural addictions, attachment and suffering.

You can find further information on Ayurveda by simply searching it on Google. This truly was a game changer for me and I hope that it may be for you.

Be the light you wish to see

By starting to take care of ourselves, watching our own language, practising self-care, shifting our self-talk, tuning into our bodies, moving well and indulging in mindfulness practices or meditation every day, we learn to listen and follow our hearts. We then offer permission to the ones around us to start to show up for themselves as well.

But if we are operating from a place of unworthiness, resentment and judgement because we are tired, people pleasing and not looking after ourselves, we are going to find that giving to another will be half-hearted and lack energy and genuine intention. It's because we are feeling stuck, immobile and exhausted, and struggling with our own sense of purpose and direction.

Remember in Story Two how Bronnie Ware stated that we are like light globes, and over time we lose our glow? This is exactly what started to happen to me at the age of six. I thought there was nothing wrong with me at all. I was vibrant, energetic, messy confident and myself. Then my belief in myself started to change when I turned someone else's words into my story. From that moment, everything I saw, watched, listened to and heard from those around me, and how I chose to see my body, started to become an uphill and never-ending battle of perfection and people pleasing. It was a slow journey of adapting for others and trying to be someone I wasn't. All because of what I was choosing to believe about myself.

What we believe starts to become our reality.

Shame and guilt are never buried

The shame and guilt from the sexual trauma that happened when I was nine was being relived every single day without my awareness. I would never feel enough and was never satisfied with what I did or achieved. I always had to perfect and perform. I adopted a failure attitude if I didn't win, or wasn't liked or invited somewhere, or didn't please my parents.

This constant belief of 'not enough' started to become so well-practised and believed that I became a shadow of myself. That's where the 'physical' manifestation of the eating disorders began. I felt I had nowhere else to go and my world had become blurred. It mirrored back to me how I was feeling about myself and I lived in a constant state of denial and self-abuse, with a sense of not being seen or heard.

This was due to my willingness to hold on to the past and choose to make it my story. Little did I know that also with my will … I was able to change it.

The chakras

Before I end this story, I would like to leave a little room for you to dive into yourself. In yoga we study the chakra system, which is best known as energy centres in the body that run along the spine. When we experience physical symptoms in the body, it is important to understand there is most certainly an underlying emotional connection. Our energy needs to flow so that we can experience equilibrium and equanimity in the mind and body.

If I were to dive into this system, it would be another book. So for the purposes of this book, I will keep it simple and to the point. Hopefully you may be able to marry up that what goes on in our minds is reflected in the body.

You can access my Clear Your Chakras course on my website at watchyalanguage.com.

I wish I was taught this in school

As a very basic guide, I'll highlight from my own teachers the relationship between the energy centres (chakras), the body and the mind.

I hope you get as much out of this as I have and spend some quality time being curious about *why* things show up, rather than judging them. For when we can see the ailment, illness, disease or injury as a blessing and a lesson, we can do something about it.

Just like these energy centres, water must flow. If we were to block a stream with debris, objects, rocks and rubbish, the water still needs to move, but it will become messy, unpredictable and backed up.

Our chakras are the same. If we are holding on to an experience (a samskara)—say, for example, that time when we lost our job—and we still feel we are unworthy or not smart enough, then it will be stored in a particular energy centre linked to that emotion.

As energy is always moving; it travels around in circles until something in our environment triggers this emotion and reminds us of how we felt ten years ago. The emotion and old story rise for us to feel them to heal them.

However, if we don't have the required tools or knowledge, we will do what we can to suppress this emotion and stuff it back down because it's too uncomfortable to sit with. This is what we call numbing or running ... as I have shared in the earlier stories.

Safe to say I was clearly up shit creek, with my stream consistently blocked—full of debris and turbulent water.

The seven energy centres

What if we ignored our kids when something went wrong? Say they have cut their foot on glass and are experiencing pain ... would we dismiss it and tell them to toughen up? Or would we do our best to remove the glass, cleanse the wound, care for them and then protect the foot? If ignored, over time the area would become swollen and infected, and of course cause more pain.

I love this simple description of the chakras from The Chopra Center:

> One of the most important things to understand about Ayurveda is how it explains your body's energy. The *chakra* system holds your body's energy (or *prana*) and your actions can help keep it in balance.

The chakra system relates to a spinning wheel of energy.

Energy centres run along our spine and they are responsible for allowing *prana* (life force energy) to flow freely. Each of the wheels (chakras) has an emotion linked to them, so if we are holding on to a samskara from our past, it will get blocked in our bodies.

Energy is always moving; nothing just goes away. So as we spoke about in earlier stories, the energy of the samskara spins around until we are triggered in our environment. It then unexpectedly, and without invitation, rises to the surface for us to either numb it again and push it back down, or choose to (do the work and) allow ourselves to feel it and heal it.

When any of the chakras are blocked, we experience a lack in energy and vitality, and can experience a physiological reaction in the body. This reaction in the body is like glass in the foot: immediately we are given a signal from our body to attend to the imbalance so that we can become aware, nurture it, and ask with compassion what it needs.

But, in the world we live in, we are conditioned to soldier on, push more and wear busy as a label, so we dismiss the bloating, the tiredness, the poor (or non-existent) digestion, the headaches and the lack of energy. These are the first signs that our wheels are falling off and if we don't acknowledge these signs, we will end up with bigger and more pressing issues, such as inflammation, autoimmune issues, sickness and dis-ease in the body.

I share the following from my online course, Clear Your Chakras, which runs as an opportunity to reset, clear the body of toxicity and gain an understanding of the link between our emotions and our body.

Muladhara—Root chakra

Colour
Red

Element
Earth

Location
Sciatic nerve roots down into the earth. Base of spine to feet

Attributes
Connection to earth, survival, health, abundance, grounding, connection.

Effects of imbalance
- You will feel an excess of Kapha energy (too much earth)
- Stuck, stagnant, unbalanced, ungrounded
- Depleted sense of self
- Loss of the ability to move forward

A blockage in the root chakra may be grief, guilt, sadness or fear. It may be an old belief patten from childhood, passed down by our parents and their parents. How we were treated as babies—nurtured, looked after or abandoned—has been programmed into our subconscious and influences how we operate our program.

Physiological effects of imbalance
- Feelings of insecurity, imbalance, loneliness, obsession, anxiety, depression
- Can't make decisions, tends towards addictive behaviour
- A lack of confidence
- Roots not anchoring down properly; too 'in our heads'

Physical effects of imbalance
- Pain in the back, groin and hips
- Diarrhoea, constipation
- Knee problems
- Sciatica
- Muscle and bone degeneration

You will also feel unbalanced in your whole body, trip over often and be unsteady on your feet.

Svadhisthana—Sacral chakra

Colour
Orange

Element
Water

Location
Coccyx, lower spine.

Attributes
Connection to others, creativity, energy, flow, confidence, sexuality, sensuality, womb, fertility, reproductive organs, the erratic energy we move through our body. Emotional realm. Pleasure or pain. Flow and flexibility.

Effects of imbalance
- Lacking energy and flow, numb, out of touch
- Using substances to numb
- Stuck, rigid, unmoving
- Body fluids are stuck and stagnant. Opposite to moving like water.
- Disconnected or addicted to sex
- Fear around sex and pleasure
- Sadness, mild depression, loneliness
- Tired, exhausted, flat, unmotivated

Physiological effects of imbalance
- Eating disorders
- Low self-confidence
- Dependency, low sex drive or too high, addictions, emotional stuckness, the ability to not feel (express emotions) maybe we were told to toughen up, or big girls don't cry? Man up?

Physical effects of imbalance
- Urinary tract infections
- Kidney function
- Chronic lumbar pain
- Imbalanced periods
- Infertility
- Genital issues

Manipura—Solar plexus chakra/navel

Colour
Yellow

Element
Fire

Attributes
Physical centre, inner strength, power, emotions, gut feelings, self-esteem, power centre. THIS IS our FIRE—where we transmute energy. Rules our digestive system.

Effects of imbalance
- Stressed, powerless to gain control
- Can't read your gut feelings, trouble with trust
- Poor memory and concentration
- Digestive issues. Thoughts, food, environment, people, relationships: all has to be digested.

- Low self-esteem and confidence
- Anger and control issues

Physiological effects of imbalance
- Fear
- Feeling uncentred
- Sugar and carb addictions
- Insomnia
- Eating disorders
- Feeling like people, environments, work and thoughts have power over us
- Feeling angry, frustrated, egoic
- High temper, righteous

Physical effects of imbalance
- Digestive issues, bloating, gut illness, indigestion
- Food allergy
- Poor metabolism
- Diabetes
- Obesity
- Acne
- Autoimmune disorders
- Inflammation from stress
- Constant judgement of the self

Anahata—Heart chakra

Colour
Green

Element
Air

Attributes
Centre of spirit, energy centre for mental, physical and

spiritual wellbeing. Love, compassion, safety, trust, adventure, forgiveness, breath, lungs, expansion or collapse.

Effects of imbalance
- Detached and unavailable
- Losing the ability to love and nurture yourself
- Losing sight of inner beauty
- Lacking love
- Forgoing compassion to self
- Looking at material items to find pleasure
- Jealous and protective, labelling or claiming of others
- Fear, uncertainty, resistance to change
- Feeling unloved
- Inability to put yourself first

Physiological effects of imbalance
- Losing faith in self and others
- Being unforgiving
- Feeling hopeless
- Finding it hard to trust
- Uncommitted and apathetic
- Low self-worth
- Low-vibrational things happen to you
- Feelings of grief, jealousy, betrayal
- Hatred of self and others

Physical effects of imbalance
- Chest and heart problems, including angina
- Breathing difficulties
- Breast issues
- Respiratory issues
- Premature ageing
- Hunched over (protection), tight shoulders, elevated

trapezius muscles
* Elbow, arm and hand pain

The heart chakra also rules the lymphatic system.

Vishuddha—Throat chakra

<u>Colour</u>
Blue

<u>Element</u>
Sound

<u>Attributes</u>
Communication, expression, freedom, leadership, responsibility, inner truth, pharynx, larynx, expansion, contraction. Responsible for the ability to speak, listen, and express yourself freely.

<u>Effects of imbalance</u>
* You feel the need to say things but you don't
* Holding in feelings and emotion
* Lacking the ability to express yourself
* Worried about what others may think
* Blocked by feelings and emotions that can't surface or be spoken
* Feeling small, unheard, not important
* Gripped by the need to be perfect or people please to be liked and accepted

<u>Physiological effects of imbalance</u>
* Nervous
* Anxious
* Stressed
* Scared

- Can't cope
- Attention-deficit disorder
- Isolation
- Sadness

Physical effects of imbalance
- Nasal and throat issues
- Jaw pain
- Thyroid issues
- Loss of voice
- Teeth issues
- Ailments of the oesophagus and tonsils
- Colds, flus, bronchitis
- Snoring
- Blocked nose

Ajna—Third eye (brow) chakra

Colour
Purple

Element
Light

Attributes
Transcends the mind, ideas, thoughts, dreams, intuition, sense of self, awareness. Pineal gland in charge of our sleep and wake rhythms. Clear thought of inner and outer worlds. Non-separation or judgement.

Effects of imbalance
- Scatterbrain, disrupted, too many thoughts
- Can't sleep, indecisive and tired
- Loss of intuition. Judgement becomes cloudy.
- Nervous

- Indecisive
- Closing off to new ideas and getting stuck in old ways
- Stuck in old beliefs of our limitations from early on
- Stuck in the daily grind. A lack of excitement going to work or hanging for Friday.

Physiological effects of imbalance
- Headaches, migraines
- Nightmares
- Personality disorders
- Learning difficulties
- Can't remember things, scattered
- Lack of connection to body awareness

Physical effects of imbalance
- Eye problems, glaucoma
- Hearing difficulties
- Spinal conditions
- Loss of hair/itchy scalp
- Dryness
- Weak, unstable
- Disordered eating
- Self-harm
- Brain complications
- Alzheimer's disease
- Parkinson's disease

Sahaswara—Crown chakra

Colour
Ultraviolet or white

Element
Ether

Attributes
Associated with God/Source/divinity (your belief), spirituality, enlightenment, connection to the Universe, imagination, awareness, and a deep sense of peace, knowing and trust that we are supported.

Effects of imbalance
- Spiritually unconnected
- Lost, living without purpose and direction
- Depression and nervous system disorders
- Anorexia
- Mental instability
- Feeling flat
- Attachment to ego, things, hoarding, stuff, labels, tags, looks, status

If many physical ailments are present in the body, the crown is likely the cause, as this affects the six energy systems and your whole being.

Physiological effects of imbalance
- Confusion
- Depression
- Epilepsy
- Mentally disconnected
- Schizophrenia
- No lust for life
- Disconnected
- Inability to be present
- Stuck in the 'should haves' or 'could bes'
- Worried about future

Physical effects of imbalance
- Dementia
- Headaches
- Neurological disorders
- Autoimmune disorders
- Sensitivity to everything
- Overweight or underweight
- Self-harm or abuse

I hope the above information is something you can refer to often and that you can get curious, not critical, about *why* things show up in our body. Along with the study of Ayurveda, I feel the chakra system is a daily guide for us to tune in, acknowledge what we find, nurture it and do something about it. What a gift!

**The more we know about the why,
the easier it is to find compassion.**

I see you, I feel you. It's OK.

Whenever I was triggered or in an experience that made me reactive, I would revert to those old feelings of not being seen and heard. The old story of not ever being enough would rise, my back would tighten, I would bloat and the emotion was shame. My response was to shut down and numb the feelings with whatever I could find. I never allowed myself to sit in it and experience the emotion for what it was. So it got stuck.

At the time of my eating disorder, I would numb my feelings by bingeing and purging. In my anxiety, I would numb my feelings with drugs or alcohol. And in my fear of not being enough, I would run from it all by smashing it out in the gym, cutting my calories to punish myself and setting a ridiculous training regime or signing up to events that were intense, such as ultramarathons and bodybuilding competitions. All to run from what I was unwilling to feel.

In my body, this amounted to feeling bloated, tense and sharp, with recurring back pain, activated traps and shoulders from tension, and no periods. I actually only started getting regular periods two years before writing this book, such was the extent of the damage I did. My hair started falling out, I couldn't poop, I had terrible breath, and I was exhausted.

The chakra system really gave me the knowledge to understand the connection between my thoughts and my physical experience.

In the online six-week Clear Your Chakras course I offer, we spend a whole week diving into each of the chakras and getting to know our bodies from the inside out.

It was an absolute game changer for me and I invite you to do your research with a curious mind and see the connections that may exist between what you are experiencing in your body and the emotions you carry.

Remember, sometimes we shy away from knowledge because we are scared to find out the why. You are better off doing the work rather than suppressing it. Otherwise you end up later in life feeling restrained from reaching the full potential of your highest self.

That will always be your choice—your practice.

I challenge you to move your body in a new way. In a way that is filled with curiosity, investigation and fun. Dance, play, crawl, get naked and jiggle in front of a mirror by yourself or with your partner. Play with yourself; get to know what feels good, inside and out. Pleasure is meant to be experienced and it is our right to embrace ourselves exactly as we are, without the need to be any different.

Self-pleasure is essential for self-love

I purchased a pleasure wand from Rosie Rees. This was a huge step for me as it had been a slow, long and somewhat painful journey embracing my sensuality as a woman. I used to think sex, having sex and feeling sexual, was shameful. That was my experience growing up. I never knew it could be so pleasurable, empowering and liberating. It is empowering to embrace yourself as you are, and allow yourself to feel immense pleasure, satisfaction and sensuality on all levels.

Tinder Tim

You think tinder is just for hook-ups? Think again!

Over the time of writing this book, I experienced a relationship like no other that evolved due to the love I was allowing for myself. I knew that my past relationships were a match to the energy that I had been putting out there myself. I hadn't believed I was worthy, therefore my partners reflected that vibration.

When I finished the first rough copy of this book, I was in Byron Bay. I closed the laptop, said a big fuck yes and thank you to the Universe for allowing this to unfold, and then said ... 'Alright, I'm ready to meet someone that matches my love for myself.'

Did I ever get what I asked for?

Never be afraid to ask for what you want!

I jumped on Tinder that afternoon and started chatting almost immediately to someone who brought me so much joy, light and playfulness. Over the next nine months or so, we grew but did not cling. We were brutally honest and spoke our truth, and we had something that was magical, but we knew that what we had was due to how we felt inside. A complete love for ourselves without the need for someone to complete us.

He held me and my dharma during the long and sometimes challenging days of developing this book, the unfolding of the pandemic, and the anxiety, stress and fear of trusting that I was on the right path.

This relationship was different. We did not need each other—we were not attached at all—but our connection was like nothing I (or he) had ever experienced. It was electric, present and powerful.

On every level, this rocked my world.

I realised that it was me who had created what I deserved. When Tim (still called Tinder Tim in my phone) came into my life, I knew that I had changed my own beliefs and dialogue around who I was, and I knew that anything and everything was possible.

We all need a Tinder Tim in our lives to remind us that we are *so* worthy of experiencing a love like no other. The one we have for ourselves.

When you experience full self-love and acceptance, you can be authentic. The people that come into your life will be a reflection of your aura. Life just becomes incredibly amazing. The way it should be.

The shame and guilt that I experienced at six years old was held in my chakra system for nearly two decades. This blockage drove my behaviours, actions and dialogue unconsciously until I was ready to heal it and move forward with love. I had to forgive my inner child and create a new belief system ... one that knew that I was worthy, enough and able to experience love.

This is why I believe that doing the (uncomfortable) work on ourselves to stop feeding the dragon of shame is so important. When we feed the dragon, we really are holding back the true potential of who we are as humans in this world.

Affirmation

I choose to release judgement of my past and investigate what compassion and forgiveness feel like in my body.

Hopefully this story can spark a thought with you that we receive a somatic experience in our bodies when we feel shame and guilt, and physically, the body will shut down in some areas.

As Rumi once said: 'The quieter you become, the more you are able to hear.'

When I feel pain in my body, can I say thank you?

Listening to our bodies is our key to finding a new way of being and embracing ourselves just as we are without trying to fix, change, judge or alter them. From this awareness and acceptance, we can then start to dive in to do the work to help them move and feel better from the inside out.

I believe that when we experience something in our bodies (that is not from direct trauma such as an accident or injury), there is most certainly an emotion attached that we may be not paying attention to.

I'm not here to be right. That's not my job. These words are here for you to investigate with an open mind and then do your own work. We are the only ones who can figure it out for ourselves and our kids.

Welcome to the next story of getting to know you on a whole new level, almost like you can see yourself for the first time.

So I pose a big question at the end of the next story, one that has significantly changed the way I see myself and my body.

What if you could choose to say thank you the next time something shows up? It is a choice, right?

The back pain is there, the bloating is there, the bad skin is there, the constipation is there. It's showing up *anyway* so it's up to us to *choose* to see it differently—yup, you guessed it: see it with love.

Notice how different it feels to approach an ailment with compassion rather than criticism. It changes the vibration, doesn't it? We soften rather than tense up. We open rather than close. We allow rather than fight.

Try this to change your dialogue around the situation:

> Thank you for showing up [insert ailment here]. I honour you. I see you and I feel you. What is it that you are trying to tell me? How can I help you?

Be compassionate rather than judgemental around the physical reaction. This is your body trying to get you to lean in, listen, be kind and do the work.

It is only from here that we can allow and create change. Get excited because this, my friend, is a game changer.

How does that even feel?

Let's go there, shall we?

A SOMATIC EXPERIENCE– IT STAYS IN THE BODY

What are you unwilling to feel?
— Tara Brach

A mind and body connection

What if it was all connected? The unexplained 'things' that pop up regularly and frustratingly in the physical body. Things such as bloating, constipation, back pain, hip tightness, chronic fatigue, digestive issues such as irritable bowel syndrome, autoimmune problems, depression, fibromyalgia, ADHD, anxiety, and eating disorders. Should I go as far as to say cancer? Just throwing it out there for your own personal inquiry.

Is this possibly something we can use to uncover some information about ourselves and the things stuck inside? Can we invite curiosity rather than critical thinking?

'You need to backbend'

These words were the start of my curiosity about why I had

become so rigid, so stuck and in so much physical pain.

Rod Cooper from The Movement Collective in Newcastle owns a fun, playful and open space practising movement. He said these words to me when I was thirty-four.

I was at the start of my work. I had just returned from Bali and I knew deep in my heart that I needed to do something different from my very practised patterns of rigidity, perfection and people pleasing. So, despite my body's immobility and my heart's resistance, it sat with me and I thought, *I wonder what would happen if I gave it a go.*

At first, I resisted it terribly. The old thoughts and stories flooded in such as, *My back will go, I'm not built for that, I'll injure myself, I might pull something,* blah, blah, blah.

Then I was able to be present.

What if? What if there is the smallest possibility that I may be able to try it out and see if I can learn something new.

I would like you to consider the thought process of choosing to see the things that show up in our bodies with compassion rather than criticism. For example, when we experience back, hip or knee pain, instead of judging it and becoming frustrated, rigid and reactive, is it possible to practice the following dialogue with ourselves?

Thank you for showing up, pain. What is it you are trying to tell me?

Then use this information and feedback from your body to do the work. Is there possibly some stuck energy present in the physical self?

Pain is real, but can we see it differently?

For many years I suffered immense lower-back pain. It would go so regularly that I was constantly nervous about hurting it again. I had bulging discs and they were constantly inflamed.

Sometimes I wouldn't get out of bed for three days.

I was consistently thinking the thoughts *I can't do that* and *My back will give way* or saying out loud to others, 'I have lower-back issues—I don't want to risk it.'

By no means am I downplaying the real pain and suffering we feel when we experience lower-back issues, but I gave it my absolute attention and energy on a very regular basis for more than ten years, to be exact. I could have used that energy much more wisely and focused on what I *could* do rather than what I could not.

I believed my back would go and it did.

Then I shifted my dialogue and thoughts to the belief that it could heal. And it did.

This is not to say that I have not experienced back pain since. When I am out of alignment, stuck in a story of financial lack or fear, or find I feel guilt or shame over something, the first sign for me is back tension. Now I recognise it much faster and I dive into the emotion behind it so that I can heal the emotion and ease my pain. You might recognise this as the first two steps of the BE HERE method. I see the back pain, I feel the guilt. Then I offer myself compassion around it—this being the third step, 'What does my *heart* need?'

And, well, that was that. It sparked a journey of breaking down my ego, letting go of how my body should look, embracing how my body feels and genuinely starting to fully love and accept my body.

Exercise is a modern word. Movement is what we do. This is where it becomes an embodied and present experience. Movement taught me more about myself, my heart and my mind than anything I had ever practised before. It took me a while to drop my walls, my goals and my belief of not being enough and fully embrace moving, playing, imperfection, curiosity and imagination through feeling into the body.

Our bodies are our biggest teachers and if we are too busy chasing a dress size, a certain goal weight, a number on a scale or the old *When I get fit I'll be happy,* we will always be searching for something that is unattainable, unrealistic and out of our reach. When we hit that certain goal, we still won't be happy and we'll search for something else. Is that truly a way to live the rest of your life? Not enjoying the moment right here, living your life in the future and missing out on what is here now?

This is it. Not when you have X, when you weigh X, what you look like or who you impress with your physical state. You could lose it all in a moment.

If we base our happiness on what we have, how we look and what we own, we will be on the constant hunt for more and never truly be happy.

Journal moment

The next time you are faced with inflammation, an injury or pain, see what's showing up in your body with compassion.

Write this down somewhere where you will see it regularly to remind you to say thank you rather than judge what you see or experience.

Thank you, pain/inflammation/or injury for showing up. What is it that you need from me today? How can I help you?

Notice how much nicer this feels in the body over anger, frustration or judgement to the area. The more you practice, the easier it becomes to offer compassion over criticism.

I hope you can gain from this chapter a better understanding of what happens somatically in the body when we experience trauma and raw emotions or suppress feelings that we are unwilling to recognise.

Emotion—from the Latin *emovere*—means to move out.

You can see how energy is stored in our bodies through the chakra system, and if they don't move, then things, quite literally, get stuck.

Charles Darwin researched the connection between humans, animals and emotions back in 1872 and published *The Descent of Man*.

He stated in this text:

> ... man and the higher animals ... have some few instincts in common. All have the same senses, intuitions, and sensations,—similar passions, affections, and emotions, even the more complex ones, such as jealousy, suspicion, emulation, gratitude, and magnanimity ...

This raises an interesting question for us as to physically what happens when we feel 'e-motion'.

- When we shut down, the same as a lizard in the midst of fear (they lose their tail), we also, quite literally, close.
- When I am anxious, I suffer from bloating.
- When I feel fear, I close my heart.
- When I experience judgement of the self or comparison, I feel tight in my heart and pain in my chest.
- When I am struggling financially, or feeling deep emotional pain, I get back pain and tightness.

- When I feel grief, my shoulders curl in and my neck tightens. I also have issues with my elbows.

On the flip side ...

- When I'm feeling empowered, my shoulders roll back.
- When I practise gratitude, I feel my face soften and my heart open.
- When I am content, my whole body is open, my mind is clear and I feel supple.
- When my heart is open, I am present and able to make good choices that affect my behaviours and actions.
- When I am in the moment and can be the observer, I can be present and respond, rather than react.
- When I am open, I am receptive and I am in flow.

Journal moment

Experiment with your family or kids the distinction between closing and opening.

Closing feels tense, shy, lacking in confidence, reactive.

Opening feels expansive, clear, confident and responsive.

From the Watch YA Language six-week online immersion

I want to share with you a table that helped me understand

when my body was in reactivity, so that I could ask myself, *Is my tension really necessary?* In ninety-nine per cent of situations, tensing up is completely unnecessary and only shuts down our nervous system.

So—notice, name it. Pause, breathe, choose again.

REACT	RESPOND
Judgement	Compassion
Aggression	Kindness
Righteousness	Choice
Blame	Awareness
Living in the past or future	Presence
Being closed	Openness
Sympathetic nervous system	Parasympathetic nervous system
Low self-esteem	Confidence
Jealousy	Acceptance
Inability to let go	Allowance
Comparison	Contentment
Autopilot	Present

This is a great exercise to do with yourself and with kids. Tune into what is going on somatically in the body, and maintain presence as you ask yourself *Is there a way I can do my best to remain open and not closed?* A closed reaction will never release tension.

**Your body will always be your biggest teacher;
we just need to learn to tune in and listen.**

This book has been such an important part of my healing process along the way and this, no doubt, was part of the journey. I have this on my blog at watchyalanguage.com.

Things always show up. They always will. We are always doing the work, but you now know you have a choice to see them differently.

I am so damn grateful for giving myself permission to experience all the feels as they came up and see what it was that I needed to learn.

Judging myself and my body's response

Saturday 27 February 2021 was the first day of our 'Weekend Intensive' for our movement traineeship at Infuse Health, Adamstown. I had been anticipating and looking forward to this weekend for a while with a somewhat nervous, curious, terrified and unsettled mind. I didn't have the best sleep leading into the day, and my food choices (and a few glasses of wine) hadn't really helped me; I woke up feeling anxious and flighty, sporting a wonderful monkey mind (this being a mind that is constantly going between what we need for dinner, our report that's overdue and what we need to pick up for our kid's birthday on the weekend).

I was aware though that I was not feeling in flow and chose to do some movement, walk the dog and have a little meditation before I went in for the first day.

During the day, I became increasingly judgemental and critical of myself. I was tensing my shoulders, my belly had bloated and my breathing had sped up. My thoughts were becoming louder and my head a little cloudier. My energy had gone from excitement to a little exhaustion and I felt flat.

I didn't notice this straight away. It took a few hours for me to register what was going on in my body and then associate it with my thinking.

When I was on the drive home I turned off the radio to tune in a little to myself and try to listen. To try to work out what was making my body react the way it was—what was causing my thoughts to move from acceptance and gratitude to comparison and judgement.

It didn't take long. We had spent a big part of the day in constructive criticism and when I paused, I was immediately taken back to my childhood years of feeling criticised, small, insignificant and not smart, fast or anything enough.

I did my best to observe this and ask the question, *Why is this presenting? What is it that needs to be felt, healed and let go?*

I investigated this further. I had no problem with accepting myself as I was; I was comfortable AF with my body by then and had no thoughts of ever embracing an eating disorder again or purging. But criticism ... this was new to me. I hadn't been in this environment in a very long time. Why was this showing up? What was this about?

A deeper dive took me back to memories of feeling embarrassed, small and not heard. In the times of my eating disorder, talking about and expressing these emotions was not as common as they are today, and I felt immense shame and guilt that I was putting my family through this. You can see this in the letters I wrote to myself that I carried this with a heavy heart right through to my early thirties, where I continued to feel shame for not having the right job, being the 'different' one in the family, and breaking the mould of the happy family upbringing.

I struggled immensely in my early thirties with concentration, reading and taking information in. I was so full in my mind that I felt stupid and unworthy, and whenever I received criticism for not being able to present words and sentences clearly, it would reaffirm this old story for me.

Feeling stupid was an old limiting belief that I had been told by a teacher in Year 3 after having the blackboard duster thrown at me numerous times through class and receiving the soul-crushing slap of the school's 'paddle' more times than one should as a schoolgirl at that age ... Recognise the samskara/block?

I practised for years the choice to be the best, to perfect, to people please and to always do better. I never really knew how to accept myself as I was. There was always something more. So whatever I did in school, in any sport, and then in my work life, I was always searching for something that was out of reach. I never felt proud, knowledgeable, or accepting of anything that I did. When I was criticised at school, home or at work, I would take it as a huge failure on my part and then the language and thoughts would start to roll.

This was purely my perspective and impression-based tunnel vision at the time. I was criticised in a way that was not constructive. It felt to me as though I could never get there, it was never enough; there was an edge of comparison and perfection with everything I put my hand to. And if I failed at the goal—which happened often because being a perfectionist means you never reach the end goal—I would then turn to self-sabotage, body abuse, cutting, gym and food addiction, or not eating.

Before I go any further, it is important to mention that this was how I chose to see the world. This was nothing that anyone else did or said. It was how I perceived the world and others words through my lens at the time of my dark, shamed and guilty heart. My parents, friends and the people around me did all they could with the tools they had at the time.

Growing up, things were easy for me and I was a spoilt and loved child. On the outside, it felt we had to hold up the image of a perfect family. However, emotions were not seen nor felt. Shame and guilt were tucked away and forgotten about. Things were scooted over and we never had real, raw and painful powwows where we could actually listen to each other, including, on a large scale, myself. And because we are mirrors of each other, this became a constant pattern of righteousness, blame and finger pointing.

I feel conversations were stopped to avoid discomfort with the family and sometimes things were not mentioned to 'keep the peace'. I even felt to a point that my eating disorder was hushed up to keep the 'normality' of the family and I also totally understand why that was done.

So, over these many years, I had learnt—through the development of neural maps—that avoidance was the way forward. But this is never the way forward as things will always pop up. Being truthful and honest and sitting in the uncomfortable is the only way we grow.

Triggered by the same story years later

So, when we were at training, and moving through the day, I was slowly allowing myself to be triggered by constructive criticism that was bringing up an old way of being. An old way that I knew so very well from more than thirty years of practising thoughts of not being enough. For years, when I felt I was criticised, I would take it all on board and move straight into self-sabotage, vomiting, overexercising, cutting or not eating for days so I could 'punish' myself for being a shitty human. Maybe you've been there too?

Somatically, my body was locking up with stress and a mountain of thoughts, and my belly had turned into a balloon. It was like I was living as I had back as a teen with huge insecurities and the mission to be the best and people please. How I hate to write down those words, but that's the awful truth. I was taken back to moments in my childhood of feeling unheard and unseen, struggling with my body while feeling embarrassed as a daughter to my mother and father.

I could have chosen to give ammo to these thoughts by getting home, feeling shitty about myself and driving to the botte shop to buy a bottle of wine.

But I didn't.

Turn your triggers into your teachers

This day was a huge teacher for me and I'm so grateful. I am also just as humbled by and thankful for my parents for doing the best they could. Without all of these experiences, there is no way I would be where I am today.

By choosing to dive into the work, remaining present and deciding to be curious not critical about what I can learn, I see the situation through new eyes. I am surrounded by the most open, loving, direct and humble people I know—people who have no problems speaking their truth from a compassionate heart. This is how we move forward and grow as humans, especially in the world we are in today where avoidance and comparison stems into body dysmorphia and modifications, alcohol and substance abuse and the constant need to look like an influencer that has been possibly edited with trimmed thighs, a twelve-centimetre waist and puppy dog eyes.

Even though I'm writing a book on authenticity and acceptance, I don't cruise on by with my shit together. Hell no. Things come up and when old stories from the past are triggered, it means the Universe is giving you permission to feel it now and heal. We are always doing the work.

But thanks to the practice I share in this book, the BE HERE method, I realised that I consciously had a choice of what to do, and I chose to investigate the messiness that was arising and sit in it with compassion and do my best to move through it. These old stories that I carry around criticism are a work in progress for me, but one that I now choose to honour; I give myself permission to forgive the inner child that believed these old stories about herself.

It is only from here that I can unlearn the old patterns and neural maps of thinking I'm a shitty person. I can slowly start to fire and wire a new neural map with the response, *When I am faced with constructive criticism, I take it as a huge opportunity to grow and learn.* Remember, our triggers are our best teachers.

I was also able to park that old story, learn from it and not judge it. By being here now, I am able to be the best I can be in this moment. And that is all that matters.

So, thank you, God, for bringing this to my attention. I am so grateful for the experience, and know there will be many more days of training that are going to push my boundaries, challenge my 'old' way of being and help me be the best person I can be— not just for myself, but for others.

You get what you wish for

Remember, we are always asking of the Universe, and if we keep reacting with a closed heart, a rigid and tense way of being and an inability to accept and yield to change, then we will get more of the same back to us.

Remember the mirror neurons we spoke about in the past story? This energy we feel is *reciprocity*, knowing that we are held safely in another's space. Being truly seen and heard by the people around us. It is also reflected between you and the person in front of you.

You can feel a sense of trust or judgement just by observing another's facial expression, the way they hold their shoulders, the crinkles at their eyes and the tone of their voice, as well as the way they are standing and whether they are puffing their chest or hanging their head. We are constantly using non-verbal language. Just like watching a movie that is in French—you can still gain an understanding by observing the way they move, their interactions, the softening or hardening of their physical self and the way they move together on screen.

This is our most primal state. An intuition and tuning in to what it is that the body needs in every single moment. We are creatures that rely heavily on one another due to our basic survival instincts and nature. When we start to tune out of our bodies and focus on the external, the things we own, the way we look, the status we hold, how many followers we have on social media and the shape and size of our waist, boobs and butt, we are living our lives in a state of need and lack, and a constant want for more.

We live in reactivity (autopilot) rather than response (presence). We forget that we already have everything we need.

Connection is who we are and it is up to you and me to bring this back in a big way in the disconnected world we live in.

What if we learnt this from an early age?

If we had the opportunity to learn about our bodies in school and how they react when we feel emotion, imagine the possibilities of compassion and awareness that could be available to us. We could learn to *respond*, not react.

I work with kids and adults. Teaching kids to practise presence is as simple as getting them to be in their bodies, which I never learnt how to do until my mid-thirties. There are now also plenty of kids' movement classes around the world that align with the principle of moving to have fun, not to achieve a certain goal, to be the best, or to strive and push for perfection.

Learning to be in our bodies rather than focus on the external is something that, when developed over time, I believe will help eliminate the self-judgement, over-striving and perfection we are conditioned into while growing up.

You can see from the earlier exercise that when we tense up, we are choosing to close. We are being triggered by an emotion. Hence the first two steps of the BE HERE method:

> I SEE you, body (shoulders tensing, fast breath, bloated tummy, closed heart).
> I FEEL you, emotion (fear, anxiety, worry, doubt, shame).

In Buddhism it's called notice and name. If you can tune into the somatic experience in your body, when you feel an emotion, you have the power to let it go.

The moment is going to be what it is. You have the choice as to how you react or respond.

Reaction will keep your body in fight-or-flight (your digestive system shut down), whereas response will keep you regulated and well, and you can remain open, even through the storm.

Check out the '5 minute breathwork practice to calm the mind' video on my YouTube account to bring yourself to presence.

Chelsea

Chelsea has had a great morning at home with her little sister and mother. She is eleven years old.

It's a challenging age for girls (and guys) at this time: they're getting into the phase of their life where they start to discover their bodies, feel more emotions and move through the awkward transition into their teens. At school, there are different groups of peers, somewhat separated by looks, sport and even educational/social standards—which already creates ripples in the system. But as we all know, this part of our growth is messy and uncomfortable—a time where we just do our best to survive, get to know ourselves, and figure out who we are and what we are about.

Conversations and hangouts usually include topics about boys, bodies, influencers, YouTube, Twitch, makeup and, unfortunately, calories, TikTok trends and dieting.

At home, Chelsea and her mum and sister have been working on practising gratitude and some affirmations as Chelsea has been feeling triggered at school lately by a few other students. They do this practice for ten minutes and Chelsea has been feeling good while practising this, and it is helping her mother as well.

However, each morning as Chelsea goes to school, the practice is forgotten and fear sets in.

Arriving at school, Chelsea feels fear, anxiety, tension and physical illness. Her tummy feels tight, she gets headaches, her body closes, she loses the ability to speak up and her body language has changed immensely since being at home. She has had an experience with other students who have bullied her, made her feel small, judged her and made her question her true authentic self, so she feels the need to people please, make others happy and change who she is in order to suit others.

Just to take it back a little here. Do you remember what I spoke about in early stories in regards to our samskaras that get stored? Chelsea has had an experience and she has not let go, and every time she knows she is going to see that person or group of girls, her mind is pre-empting the situation and how she will be treated.

If Chelsea were present and able to be in the moment, she could possibly create a different outcome by becoming aware of her mind and her body.

Physically, her body tenses and tightens up, her shoulders roll inwards, her chest closes around her heart, her head lowers, she feels sick in her belly and her voice starts to tremble. Chelsea's state of mind is also affected. She is now feeling distracted, agitated, judgemental, and critical of herself.

She has just moved from her ventral vagal state (social engagement, and positive states of relaxation) to her spinal sympathetic chain (fight or flight). There are some stories swimming around in the background along the lines of, *I feel unworthy, I am different, Why don't they like me?* or *I'm not enough ... will I ever feel accepted?*

In this short space of time, not only has Chelsea's energy changed, but her physical structure has become a shadow of what it was when she was at home practising gratitude, compassion and appreciation for the things she has, including time with her family.

If Chelsea were able to, in the moment, acknowledge what was going on, she may have had a chance to catch it and do something about it. She would also have been able to keep her autonomic nervous system (recognising that when someone judges us, they are coming from a place of unworthiness themselves, she would have also been able to regulate her nervous system to maintain social engagement and feel compassion for the other) in a state of ease. This is extremely important for our overall wellbeing and health, and for maintaining an open presence.

Things happen very fast as we know, and the moment can unfold very quickly.

If Chelsea were able to recognise the emotions and physical signs, this is where she could create change and start to practise kindness and compassion for herself instead of having a repeat of the same situation.

This is why, in the BE HERE method, the body is the very first thing we pay attention to. Kids are very tuned into their bodies and know that when the body is open, they feel confident, happy and kind, and when it closes, they feel anxious, scared and small.

One thing I share with kids is this: You are always able to see others and a situation as if for the first time. Whatever is being thrown at you in the schoolyard is from the other person's pain. We never bully if we feel love or compassion for ourselves. If we don't feel love for ourselves, this gets taken out on others.

You can choose not to take it on board by being light instead. Choose to open your heart, pull your shoulders back, hold your head high and breathe. This response will also be a mirror image to those around you and whatever anyone says or does is not personal, unless we choose it to be. Give kind, receive kind.

The family Christmas party ... need I say more?

Did you feel your body tense a little?

Ever felt the pangs of anxiety and fear sometimes weeks before the staff or family Christmas party, dinner with the in-laws, or the work meeting where so-and-so makes you feel triggered?

Already we are creating a story in our mind—losing our sense of presence. And by constantly thinking about how terrible it's going to be when we get there, see this person or attend the meeting, guess what it is we are going to create?

All of us have been in this situation at one point or another—whether it be at home with family, parents or siblings, at school or college, or in a work environment—where we are triggered by a moment that hasn't even happened yet and we get a somatic response in our bodies.

This is your key to understanding the connection between your thoughts, your words and how your body is reacting to the way you think and speak. It is not rocket science, and it is not new. Your body will be your biggest teacher, but it also involves just as much awareness of the heart and the mind to pick up on what you are putting down.

So, the next time you find yourself creating Mount Everest with your thoughts and a bull at a gate with a story, you need to ask yourself the question: *is this necessary and how does this make me feel?* If it's making you feel anxious, fearful or small, then there is your work. Your work is to be present, pause, and choose again. Remember, you have the ability to create a new story. It starts with a new choice, which creates a new experience.

Then practise the shit out of that. Rome was never built in a day.

Balance is key

Ayurveda has been around for approximately five thousand years. It is simple and easy to understand. It is described as 'the science of life'. It is based on the belief that health and wellness depend on a delicate balance between the mind, body and spirit.

Balance, I believe, is how quickly we can bring our bodies and minds back to equanimity. To move through our day and not cling to or resist the moments we experience.

Traditional Chinese medicine is the same. If focuses on *jing*, your essence, your foundational structure from birth; *shen*, your spirit, awareness, mental health and connection to your heart; and *qi*, the energy between that moves the two—the breath, attitude and space you have to be present.

If any of these are out of balance, your qi energy will not flow. Things get stuck and you feel tired and exhausted; lack self-esteem, awareness and abundance; and are judgemental and constantly searching for more.

In my online coaching, I show it is important to make sure we look at all three elements for good health, vitality and acceptance—mind, body and spirit (heart). You can also join my Free Your Flow course, now offered online, as a fourteen-day guide to understanding with compassion the things that block our energy. This covers the basics of Ayurveda, as well as our samskaras and what we can do about them! You can find the course on my website at watchyalanguage.com/onlinecourses.

Journal moment

Grab your journal the next time you or your little one are experiencing emotions and see if you can kindly label what you are experiencing using the BE HERE method.

- *I see you, BODY.* Label the physical sensations going on.
- *I feel you, EMOTION.* Write them down.
- *What is it that my HEART needs?* Tune in and answer.
- *I'm now EMPOWERED with knowledge.* What are you grateful for that you have learnt along the way? I know the difference between REACTING and RESPONDING:
- Reactivity looks like …
- Response looks like …
  I choose to shift my ENERGY to be the light I wish to see.
- The energy I choose to radiate today is …

Taking running (and numbing) to a whole new level

At thirty-three, I was mentally unstable. I was working as a marketing and graphic design manager for a health club in Newcastle, coming off the back of an equally busy national radio position, where there was the constant drive for higher sales, more money, more status and of course, more work. This was highly addictive for me. I had spent most of my twenties drinking, taking drugs and partying—all the time battling bulimia and body dysmorphic disorder. I was at a point where I couldn't continue to numb myself with the party drugs, so I worked my arse off instead.

The media industry pushed me to my mental limits—I was constantly chasing a number and figure—and the anxiety heightened the more my pay soared. This by no means was a terrible job. It definitely had its perks. But the state of mind I was in—after not allowing myself to feel the pain of my own emotions, feelings and heart that was craving love and attention—landed me in a very messy state of confusion, with low self-esteem, no clarity and a power struggle with my ego to prove to everyone that I had my shit together.

I also was struggling with my body hugely as burnout had started to take its toll. The effects of the previous ten years—including all the sitting that comes with working in radio—were starting to show. Whenever I was triggered and unstable thoughts of my body came into my head, I would take to the bathroom and vomit back up my lunch, or overeat at night and spend the next hour or two purging it all up, leaving me with lack of sleep, no energy, bad skin and brittle hair. I'm very grateful to this day that I still have healthy teeth and gums.

When I was offered a position in health for a fitness club, I took it with the intention of getting my life on track, and expected I would be so much better.

Changes cannot be made externally to fix what our heart desires. We must search within and work from the inside out.

I started five days a week but again shifted into the same patterns and conditioning, staying back to meet deadlines, rushing to get work done, completing design work from home and addressing emails late at night—sometimes on my phone at 2:00 am when I couldn't sleep. Nothing had changed, and my mind was slowly deteriorating.

Through that time I started doing more personal training. I was always teaching exercise classes, and had been from nineteen. Sometimes I taught up to nine Les Mills classes a week. I was constantly learning choreography and giving one hundred per cent of my energy to bounce around on stage with weights, on a bike or in a functional format.

I was cooked. Mentally. Physically. Emotionally. No concentration, couldn't sleep, couldn't read, fumbled sentences. Yet I was still searching for escape from the dark feelings in my heart that I had been conditioned to suppress and not feel. This was happening subconsciously; I had no idea about emotions and that they were meant to be felt. Being busy all the time, for me, was a cover for the energy that was trying to come up and present itself.

Downstairs one day in the change rooms, one of our trainers at the gym mentioned she was running again in Comrades, a ninety-kilometre ultramarathon in South Africa (this was her tenth time). Straight away I was like, 'I can do that! When is it, and what do I need to do?'

From there I embarked on a six-month training regime of gruelling summer runs all around Newcastle, up hills and through the bush, to get myself ready for this incredible event held in Durban.

It didn't even occur to me at the time that I had chosen to do this to again numb and run from the painful emotions of shame, guilt and blame that I was so tightly holding on to because of the belief that I was never enough. I thought if I did this, I would feel enough. People would be proud of me and I would feel complete.

On a side note, this race was incredible. I'm so very grateful for that conversation in the change room and my determination to give this a go. I have never experienced anything like it and despite the battles I was having with my mental health, I appreciated it for what it was: an incredible experience running with some amazing humans, some of whom had done this event up to twenty times. For the whole race, families greeted us with the biggest smiles and cheers to get us through this gruelling uphill battle of pure grit and determination. There were stalls, barbecues and dancers. That race was the start of my teachings of gratitude, humility and appreciation, but I didn't know it at the time.

And for the record, yes, I finished it in ten hours and fourteen minutes. But was I happy?

No.

In fact, the bubble burst for me almost as soon as I finished. I thought that by completing Comrades I'd feel proud, content, happy and alive. Instead, I felt empty. Real empty, and I was back on the comparison train—*Why didn't I do better?* See the familiar pattern here?

After Comrades, and after I could walk again (which did *not* happen quickly), I set myself a new goal: a bodybuilding competition. I was now working for a personal training company in Newcastle, and I was back on the 'busy train'.

I still had not broken the destructive pattern

With up to fifty half-hour personal training sessions per week, plus Les Mills classes and my own training, I was on a sinking ship. My energy was slowly starting to drop. I was moving to punish my body as I was eating shitty food, and then sometimes bingeing, as I was trying to preserve energy to give to others.

At some point, I was searching, again, for something external to make me feel better. I became adamant that I would prove to myself that my eating disorder was over. And I would do a fitness competition to have the experience of being totally OK with my body at any weight. I had started to research the connections between my use of the app MyFitnessPal, bikini competitions and eating disorders, and was doing so, apparently, purely out of interest. Again, in hindsight, I was numbing. The self-sabotaging thoughts were getting really loud by this point. I was thirty-four and it was the loudest the noise had ever been in my head. It was like a consistent chatter of backwards and forwards voices that were always trying to figure out, fix or skim over the reality of what was going on.

Exhausting.

The comparison felt like it was constant, the judgement was never-ending and the strive for perfection was always in the back of my mind.

So I embarked on another journey of eight months of training, dieting, calorie counting and, essentially, numbing. Here we go again.

Fast forward eight months. Picture a water-deprived, leather-looking, orange, skinny, hard-as-rock, nervous and perfection-driven me. Standing on stage, dizzy from lack of water, feeling sick from a two-day immersion in fake tan, in less sparkly blue material than what you would find on a doll, trying to balance in stilettos. Yeah, it was a not-so-glamorous experience.

It is worth mentioning that I had an incredible coach at the time who guided me as healthily as possible through this experience.

Again, I am definitely proud of what I achieved and the dedication I put in to make this happen, but after it had finished, where was the feeling of satisfaction? Happiness and acceptance? Hadn't I just created the perfect body from all angles? Wasn't I the perfect image of fitness and strength? What more could I have wanted now that I had stripped my whole body of its essential fat (and suppleness).

Of course I wanted more. And this is where it became overwhelming.

Because the body is so deprived, most participants after these comps stack on the kilos straight away and in a very dangerous manner. A danger for the body and for the mind, for which I guarantee no one is prepared.

No matter how much you hear the words, 'Make sure you reverse diet slowly—take your time, but be prepared to put weight back on,' after eight months of seeing a different body than what it had been, guess what? You have now created something to compare to—this tiny, muscly, ridiculously toned and unrealistic version of yourself that absolutely cannot be maintained for many health reasons.

As I moved through those final two weeks, I dropped a lot of weight and my body changed as I started to really limit my calories and water intake. This state nearly set me back into my eating disorder as my thought process started to become, *Go you. Look how determined and controlled you are. I wonder if you can drop lower?* My weight got quite low, which at the time I was secretly celebrating. But I knew deep down that I was in a danger zone.

When we lack self-care we are at risk of the old stories.

The moment I start to move out of alignment, eat foods that don't nurture my body, don't get enough sleep, and choose to self-sabotage, my brain quite quickly goes back to what it knows well. And if we have practised patterns for more than thirty years, we can be at risk of lighting up these old, well-driven neural pathways to trigger old stories and beliefs. If we go back to the Hand Model of the Brain, our reptilian brain, our basic survival needs are food, sleep, sex, peeing, pooping, shelter and digestion. If these are out of whack, we will be too.

Neurally, I was starting to fire and wire thought patterns that were so familiar. The thoughts of not feeling enough as I was, that I needed to lose weight to be accepted and that I needed to look a certain way to feel worthy were all I started to think about. And—if we remember the principle of neuroplasticity— what fires together, wires together. I was really starting to collapse back into a very practised and familiar way of thinking.

Isn't it about time we started to do the work to shift our dialogue and create a new story?

We have been trained to believe that we are not good enough as we are. There is a belief that there is something lacking, or something we need to perfect or perform, or something we need to fix.

We will be fine when we are more lovable and acceptable. We have this belief that we must become smarter, skinnier, younger, richer and sexier, get married and have children, and have the white picket fence and high-paying career. It's the constant climb up the ladder to create … you know, success.

To fit in with society, we feel we must get validation from social media on how impressive the size of our engagement ring is, how our body looks in 'that' photo, or the abundance of the kids' party we have just held. We yearn to impress our friends by enlarging our lips, losing weight, buying the right brand of activewear, or dating the guy that's untouchable at the gym.

We can sweat away a lifetime on a treadmill only to touch the surface layer. What we realise is that no matter how many calories we burn, or how many hours we train, the feelings are still present under the layers. It's now time to surrender, embrace what it feels like to simply love the skin we are in, accept that we are here due to our choices and words, and realise that to heal the internal, we must do the inner work, the hard work. And the outer will follow.

Surface-level satisfaction will get us nowhere if we keep hovering above what we are unwilling to feel.

The thoughts started to present in my body

It was not long after the event that I really started to go downhill, deeper than I had ever gone, where it was darker than I had ever seen. I was only seeing grey and my belief in myself had become non-existent. I ploughed myself into more work, more training—of course, to lose the extra kilos I had gained after the comp—and more attempts to make my life worthy, while slowly but surely slipping into a dark place that I had no idea how to run from.

About five months later, feeling the effects of poor body and brain hygiene, my body could not take the numbing and running anymore. I was churning through up to ten clients a day, restricting food, filling the space by overtraining, overworking and constantly doing, sloshing myself with alcohol to numb the pain. My brain was clogged, messy and cluttered and I was sleeping about four hours a night. My skin was pasty, hair thin and breaking, gut bloated constantly and periods still absent.

It had to come to a head.

As I left for work one morning at 5:00 am, I drove directly in front of an Aldi truck. I was so unclear that I am unsure if this was on purpose, or I was just that exhausted and in a state where I gave no fucks whatsoever that I went through the motions.

There is power in the pause

In that time of pause, on the side of the road, reeling as to what had just nearly taken place, I surrendered and broke down. I needed change, but I had no idea where that was going to come from, or what I needed to do.

I prayed. God did I pray. I prayed to whoever was listening for a guide to help me out of this life that I had created.

Luckily, the Universe had it all sorted for me. All I had to do was trust, listen and receive.

Journal moment

- When have you found yourself numbing and running from emotions? Note this in your journal.
- What happens in your body when you feel judgement, comparison, fear, doubt, and worry that you're not enough?
- What happens in your body when you feel gratitude, love, compassion, kindness and acceptance?
- What is it that you are unwilling to feel?

Next time you are faced with a situation that is uncomfortable—name in your journal—are you able to sit with it and see if you can observe what goes on in your body, and in your mind.

Emotions that are unfelt or unaddressed will lay dormant until something in our environment triggers them. Our triggers are our teacher to let it come up with compassion, curiosity and courage to see what we can learn from this experience.

I CHOOSE TO CHANGE THE ENVIRONMENT

Our beliefs do not define us. In fact,
they can make us stronger if we
choose to see it as a part of our ride.

I was lucky enough after my near accident to have been gifted time to pause. I broke down—or as Brené Brown calls it, I had a 'spiritual awakening'—and was able to take some time out to head to Bali.

It had been so long since I had paused, stopped and been with my thoughts, body and emotions that it all came crashing in and I started to see clearly.

I went from training fifty clients each week, teaching nine classes and working out every day to a space of sleeping in and walking in tropical lush nature. I started to *practise* yoga for the first time in my life.

I had been one of those practitioners who went to yoga to burn calories, sweat and push and push and push. Bali taught me there was something deeper. My soul started to connect and

I started to feel that it was so much more than the physical.

My body started to heal over these ten days. I went from a very sick, fluid-filled, post-bikini-fitness-competition body to a body and mind that were finally getting what they needed. To stop.

Bali was my pause button, my key to observing the thoughts, words and behaviours that I had chosen up to this point, and the make-or-break time to do something about the situation I was in.

Bali gave me a choice.

I decided to find out what was underneath these patterns, addictions, behaviours and choices so that when I returned to Australia, I would not fall back into being the same human that I was.

There was no way I was going to allow that to happen.

I had to choose. And I knew I had to do the work.

So I prayed.

I asked for help. And help flew my way quicker than my dog to her dinner.

I had to change my environment, and it was going to be a big job, but I was ready. Fuck was I ready.

Little steps at a time

Dr Joe Dispenza says: 'If your thoughts can make you sick, is it possible that your thoughts can make you well?'

The practice of gaining knowledge on my brain, nervous system and the body/mind connection was a game changer for me. It was the work of Dr Dispenza, Dr Dan Siegel, Dr Bruce Lipton and Dr Masaru Emoto that gave me a sense of hope that maybe if I could change the way I spoke to myself, I could possibly (one day) see myself in a new light.

I needed to understand why I continued to choose the same reactive patterns each time something happened in my environment and my buttons were pushed—such as when I would have a conversation with family, end up in a toxic relationship, feel small at work, receive a comment on my social media or feel judged around new people or a social scene.

What I was seeing was a reflection of my own energy. This whole book is a reflection of what I experienced in my mind, not what anyone else has done or said.

The reality of judgement

We are always a mirror to what we are seeing in front of us. If I was feeling unworthy or not enough around my family, it was because I was feeling that about myself. If my relationship was toxic, it was because of the energy I was putting out. If I felt small at work, it was because I wasn't fully backing myself. And if I felt judged by comments on my social media, it was because I was still judging myself and my actions.

I believe if we can become the observer of the situations that unfold around us, and what we are experiencing in our bodies and in our minds, we can tune in and choose again.

When we become present and observe the fact that we feel small, we feel judged, we feel unworthy, we feel not enough—it is a juicy piece of information that there is something in our own hearts that we need to take care of. This is a blessing in disguise.

My amazing friend and coach Cathy Feenan says: 'When we are given challenging moments from God we are receiving a blessing ... a blessing and a lesson.'

When we judge another, we are saying more about ourselves than the person we are judging. Don't judge your judgement: instead, dive in, do the work. It is your soul that needs self-love.

Challenges can teach us to tune in. When we judge another, we need to fill our own hearts with compassion and acceptance and come back to doing the work.

Our body, our heart and our soul are reaching out for our attention in these moments.

Read that again if you would like to. I am still reminded of this all the time, and I am getting much quicker at responding not reacting to situations that unfold, and truly asking myself, *What am I choosing to see right now? How does it feel in my own heart to believe this story?*

This is mindfulness in a nutshell. Easy to talk about, hard to put into practice.

But I promise you, with practice, repetition and awareness, you will see the changes yourself over time.

We are the product of our thoughts and words.

Growing up, I never really had tools to deal with what I felt. I don't remember emotions and feelings being discussed (they likely were, but I was so far gone I chose not to hear) and if they did come up it just ended with me blaming myself, getting angry or frustrated and then self-sabotaging. And because this was so well-practised, every time I felt something I would numb it, run from it, and then shoot myself in flames as I had no other program in my brain to make a better choice.

This is never anyone's fault. We all go through life experiencing it the way we see it. Others around us do the best with the tools supplied to them. It is up to us and us only to change the way we see our environment. All of the journey along the way is part of becoming who we are.

Over the years, in my own life and through my work with others, I have observed that this reaction of numbing and running from our thoughts and feelings is very well practised in society. We have been conditioned to believe that if we suppress our feelings, one day they will magically disappear. We have been trained to present ourselves as though 'we have our shit together' and 'to soldier on'.

The words 'I'm fine' clearly come with the energy of the complete opposite. Saying 'I'm fine' when we are resentful, angry, judgemental or disappointed is just a learned and practised habit that we need to start working on. This avoidance of the truth is our undoing and where we start to get stuck. We learn that by ignoring our feelings and emotions, we can present to the world that things are 'normal' and 'accepted' and that we are 'keeping it together'.

Please start to talk about the things that are uncomfortable. It's more uncomfortable to keep them in—now I hope you can understand why.

Take a moment ... is there anything that you feel you need to voice with your loved ones? Write down how you could approach this with compassion.

From a male point of view

Recently, I decided to start my press handstand journey to learn more about myself. As mentioned previously, movement is constantly reminding me to be humble, accepting of meeting myself where I'm at, and just so grateful about the fact that I can give the thing a go.

To this day, the humility that I feel being able to move the way I do will *never* be lost on me. It is so far from where I was and I will always be forever indebted to my movement teachers for sharing this incredible practice with me, completely shifting the way I see my body, movement and health.

This practice alone can seem very physical, aesthetic and 'goal' based. My experience however has been quite the opposite, which is why I have so much respect for the practice for teaching me to enjoy the ride.

I had a conversation with one of our movement teachers, Lochie Simpson, about the images we can portray on social media and what may seem accepted as a post or how it will be received by others. It's easy to get caught up in how our Instagram feed 'should' look, myself included here. We talk to audiences that follow us for the same/similar interests. So when our captions reflect vulnerability, emotional experiences or anxiety, it is easy to allow fear to get in the way of our faith, and worry what others may think and how this may be received.

Lochie is a strong, capable and stereotypically 'fit' and is not the first male I have spoken to who has struggled to have real talk on his social media page. Men are also faced with the challenges of body editing apps, where they can add muscles, sixpacks and broad shoulders at the click of a button.

However, guys like Lochie, I believe, are changing the game. Showing that strong is not just physical. It's about leaning in, showing that you feel pressure, judgement and comparison, and that it's OK not to be OK. Again, we need to choose to see it differently. Validation must come from ourselves, not from others.

We must start to see that all emotions are meant to be seen

and heard, and this applies to everyone. It's not about just glorifying the goodness that we tend to see on the highlight reel; it's just as much about the other side as well and normalising the challenging moments.

I believe it is about changing the environment of what we are seeing on our feeds, in our workplaces and in our social circles as well as old family or social conditioning patterns that have taught us for years that we need to present the best side of ourselves. To show our vulnerable or softer side is seen as weak. This is something I believe that is slowly changing in the men's world. The more we talk about depression, anxiety, expectations and body image in men, the more our population can lean in and yield to their own feelings and emotions that have been bottled up from years of comparison, perfection and not feeling enough.

Emotions that are kept in and suppressed, and the constant dialogue of 'I'm fine' or the more old-school 'She'll be right, mate' is killing us and creating rigidity, unease and tension that equates to illness, inflammation and poor mental health.

Cut the crap on being fine

The reality of 'being fine', as I'm sure you can see, is in fact a lie that we continue to tell ourselves. Of course, as I keep banging on about, what we are practising is what we are growing. If you keep telling yourself this story that you are fine all the time, your brain will start to consistently practise avoidance of feelings and emotions and immediately suppress them and they will start to store in your body and create a physiological response.

In *The Body Keeps the Score*, Bessel van der Kolk breaks down the guts of our suffering. All of us go through trauma. Not all of us allow ourselves to feel the emotions and let ourselves release the trauma so we can heal.

Your body will tell you what's going on if you can be quiet enough to listen. Tense shoulders, bloating, distraction, sleep issues, digestive problems, autoimmune disorders, anxiety, chest breathing, inflammation, skin issues, poor gut health ... the list goes on. These are sure-fire cues from your body that you need to tune in and do the work.

We are always doing the work.

What if you change the environment?

Back in the late 1970s there was a series of studies carried out into drug addiction by Canadian psychologist Bruce Alexander at Simon Fraser University.

At the time of the studies, rats were placed in a space with only water-laced heroin or cocaine. The rats had nothing else bar this in their cages and almost certainly over time were choosing the morphine water, overdosing and dying.

Alexander observed these studies and raised the possibility that if maybe the environment changed in these cages, there would be more stimulus for these rats to choose differently.

This is where he created the 'rat park', a fun playpen scattered with loads of creative things for the rats to do. They had stimuli such as toys, cheese, friends, food balls, tunnels and wheels. The rats had space to play, eat, have sex and connect. This was tested and studied to see if the rats would still choose to have the drug-laced water.

While they did partake in the drug water every now and then, there was not one overdose or death. The rats were stimulated with connection in more ways than one.

This indicates there is a strong link between addiction and connection—that when we change our environment, our behaviours change.

Something had to change

On return from Bali after my much-appreciated breakdown, I started yoga teacher training. I quit my job as a personal trainer, and launched into my study of the brain, neuroplasticity, and how to regulate the nervous system. I took a deep dive into what I had avoided all this time.

After twenty-eight years of lived-in trauma, many eating disorders and thirty years of avoidance patterns as a well-practised 'number and runner', I can confidently say that I have a good understanding of the connection between our thoughts and our body's reaction. You can get there too. It feels amazing to understand and *get to really know your body*. That's when you can start to up the self-love.

When we change our environment and start to think differently about ourselves, our whole life begins to change. It is said we are the five people we hang around—that is our environment. Studies such as those mentioned in this book show that when we choose to be present in our environment and pay attention to how it is making us feel, we are able to choose something else that actually makes us feel good. If your social media account, friends, partner or workplace is keeping you in self-sabotage, comparison, judgement or constant people pleasing, then you alone are the one who holds the willpower to choose again and again and again.

Nothing changes if nothing changes. It is not easy. This is not a six-step process for enlightenment. That is not what we are here for. It is a lifelong practice of always doing the work.

We will get tipped off balance constantly, so stop searching for the light at the end of the tunnel and get curious about the darkness that embraces you along the ride.

Choosing the path that challenges us feels uncomfortable and unfamiliar, and we will experience fear. It is up to us to lean into that fear and see what may be on the other side.

It's easy to stay the same, but if staying the same is what you are looking for then you would not have read this far. The work you will continue to do on yourself for the rest of your life will be your guide forward. Let yourself receive, give back to yourself as much as you give to others, and start to see your own vibrancy, energy and love light up.

When we start to shift and change our energy, not only do we start to feel better, but we attract more of the good stuff. I could spend a full book writing about this and share tools on this in the Watch YA Language coaching programs.

I realised I had a choice. But I had to pause to be present and aware that I was creating a life that was going to keep me stuck in my behaviour if I did not do anything about it. For me, I had to break these patterns to be driven by the fear of staying the same. My environment had to be the backbone of change.

> Pain pushes until the vision pulls.
> — Michael Beckwith

By choosing to learn about my brain and my nervous system, and that I was able to respond or react in any situation, I started to slowly make neural changes, weakening the strong synaptic cluster of self-sabotage, judgement and 'not enough' that had formed in my brain. Day by day I created new neural pathways, forming a cluster of compassion, kindness and—above all—acceptance in this brain of mine.

Journal moment

Take some time to have a look at your environment and how it makes you feel.

1. Family
2. Work
3. Gym
4. Friends
5. Social media
6. TV
7. Relationships (including the self)

Write down some notes on what each one brings up and how it makes you feel. If you are writing down more negative than positive experiences from your environment, it might be a sign for you to tune in and see what you can change to create a healthier space.

You are not here to be liked by everyone.

Not everyone is going to like what you do.

You are not here to please everyone.

So get ready to shake things up a little.

Get ready to let go and start to *put yourself first!*

It will be uncomfortable, it will be unpleasant, and you will feel pressured to continue with the old you. Again, it's up to you if you are happy to stay the same, or ready for change.

Stepping out of a regular-paying job to becoming a yoga teacher was a big thing for my family. Not just my immediate family, but also extending to my nan and others who were 'worried for my future'.

This was not particularly the 'real job and successful career' that can carry over from conditioning of what we know. Both my gorgeous parents know that my heart is fully behind what I do and support me now one hundred per cent, for which I'm so very, very grateful.

'So, what else do you do for work?'

This question amuses me immensely. I still get asked it all the time. 'So, you teach yoga and movement? How lovely. That's great. What else do you do?'

I choose to do what I love and follow my dharma, my purpose. I encourage you to look into following this deep intuitive sense that is within all of us, to one day deliver our cargo, give back and serve.

My dad, Ian, is and always will be a beautiful teacher, a mentor and my rock. It's not been easy, but there is no way that I would be here now if it were not for his teachings, love and support.

I had battled with the *What else do you do?* conversation for years with my dad, as choosing to go against the grain and teach yoga, share movement and write books was quite the opposite to what was 'normal' or accepted in the family (at the time). This concept of what's 'acceptable' is not wrong or right: we only know what we know.

One day, when we were going head-to-head in the kitchen about work, I was able to observe at some point that we were just spinning the same record on repeat: conversations would come up about my work, then the hurtful words (from both of us), and the feelings of regret, sadness and (for me) 'not good enough'. I dragged my heels out of the house as I had just witnessed again a repeat of the old dialogue, story and movie that played every time this conversation was held. I felt lost. But, this time round, I also realised I had a choice.

With the work that I had started to do on myself to practise awareness and presence, I realised that if I wanted to get a different result in a similar situation, it would have to come from me. I thought, *I wonder what could change it. Maybe I could create a different outcome; maybe I could speak up.*

I walked back in with my head held high and said a little prayer: 'Please, God, allow me to speak from my heart and let it be felt with love.'

Dad and I met in the garage. I dropped my shoulders, opened my heart, and spoke from a place of love. From deep within my heart these words spilled out: 'Thank you for your support and love, but I choose to do this for me and not for you. You can either support or acknowledge what I do, or you can choose not to. Either is fine and I love you.'

When I shifted my energy to the belief that I could do this, the energy changed between us. Our relationship has blossomed so much, and I feel the connection between us is stronger than it ever has been. I didn't know the why or how at the time, or what I was actually working towards, and it was terrifying, but I had faith that God was directing me exactly where I needed to go. I never knew it could feel this good.

Watching my dad spend the majority of his life in a job that was there to pay the bills, to provide for and support the family, made me question inside, *is it possible to one day, really do what I love? To be creative, to express myself and to be free of the nine-to-five?* And for that I am so very grateful.

He worked hard. Day in, day out, just working to put food on the table, pay the bills, pay my expensive school fees at the time, and look after the family. He didn't seem to love it, I'm sure he enjoyed bits of it, but I saw a different story—one that exhausted him, made him short-tempered and run from the hard stuff. He did it all for us and I have so much appreciation for his dedication to providing a stable and sound upbringing.

No one could have changed what went on in my own mind, what unfolded for me, was what I chose to see and believe. I was loved fully by both my parents, and blessed with all that was offered to me. My thoughts, my dialogue and my behaviours were all due to my own decision to believe a story that wasn't even mine at six years old.

Breaking the mould

When I was in the depths of my eating disorder, it became apparent that, for my family, this was increasingly difficult for them to accept or face. It would have been so hard for them to watch my health decline under their nose, without being able to do a single thing about it.

Dad, being the father figure in my life, would have felt so helpless. Due to a long career as a naval architect, his brain fires very much in the analytical, orderly, logical and linear brain. This is also known as the left brain. This is why I feel it can be hard for some parents or carers to accept or understand disordered eating, as the logical side of the brain can find a solution—*Why can't they just eat?*

As we now know, an eating disorder runs much deeper than that. So, if we can't fix it, or help, we tune out and feel disconnected and helpless in these situations.

This is where, I believe, communication is key. Talking about our emotions and feelings, however uncomfortable, unfamiliar and terrifying this may be, can help bridge these gaps of understanding between parent and child.

When we can't help or fix someone or something, we can feel inadequate, especially if our conditioning has made us feel we need to be a provider and giver. This again brings us back to numbing. This can be anything from work, to alcohol, online addiction, smoking, exercise, food or no food.

The more we run from the pain, the more we lose connection with ourselves and others. We literally become numb.

Visualise a cartoon ostrich for a moment ... one that's burying its head in the sand to avoid danger in the hope it will go away. But the problem is still there, and it's probably even bigger than before. We have all done this at some stage in my life ... I did it for those twenty-eight years. I ran from what I didn't want to feel.

This avoidance pattern is something that I see often, especially in many years of coaching, when it comes to how we deal with unpleasant unfoldings around us, especially with our loved ones. The research suggests that this stems from our upbringing and how our parents or carers dealt with their own struggles and emotions; if this has not been healed, it will be passed on through the generations.

Dr Siegel and Dr Tina Payne Bryson, in their book *The Power of Showing Up*, share the science behind these patterns, and explore how 'parental presence' can be achieved even if there is a history of avoidance patterns in the family. This involves the willingness to make sense of and reflect on our own story and attachment history—choosing to investigate our upbringing so that we can understand with compassion our own behaviours, actions and patterns, 'breaking the mould' so to speak, so that they are not passed down to our own children.

> Making sense of one's life empowers parents
> to have the open, receptive awareness of
> presence that enables them to show up
> reliably for their children.
> — Dan Siegel and Tina Payne Bryson,
> The Power of Showing Up

So, let's do our best to start the conversations—to become aware of the numbing or avoidance patterns without blame or judgement, acknowledge the fear around it, and dive in to see if we can create a different outcome for all generations to come.

Remember, we are all just doing the best we can with the tools we have, until we know better.

Worry gets us nowhere fast

I grew up in a traditional Western family that had the staple SAD (standard Australian diet), watched the news, read the papers, followed what was 'right', didn't question much, and did what other Western families did. It wasn't bad; it was just what we knew.

I worried about everything though: what was going to happen to the world, how my actions would affect my future, what others thought of me, and how I could consistently be a better person, and be validated for that ... Did it get me anywhere? No. And I bet worry has done nothing for you either.

When I started to follow my heart and trust my intuition, I did feel through this transition that I was bucking all the expectations of the family with my choices to be what I am today: a person who chooses to live from my heart space. I had a gut feeling for many years that I was going to be different.

But I knew deep down I had to trust my gut and do it anyway. It took me many years to really *believe* that I was able to follow my dream and do what I love. It's all part of the journey.

This was just my experience and how I *interpreted* those years, and I still did not believe I was worthy at the time. Like a mirror, we are always reflecting our own emotions, feelings and vibrations onto others. Of course, I was feeling judged, small, compared and a failure.

I battled with this for years, being over thirty and not married, renting, not owning a home, never holding down a secure job or salary, not having kids, and deciding to be more open on my views. Yoga and Buddhism were almost thought of as a religion in my family, and for a long time were a big topic of worry that I was, as my mum put it one day after a few wines, 'losing the plot.'

That conversation spent years in my body. It shook me and it hurt my heart. Of course, the (repetitive) story behind it was one of unworthiness and disappointment of not making them happy or proud of me. This of course, being my own limiting belief, had nothing to do with what my mum said. She triggered something that I had not healed. Those words spoken were just a passing comment, but it was how I interpreted it that was the issue.

It's up to us if we make it personal.

As we have explored, if we have not yet healed an old limiting belief or story, it will trigger the emotion and bring it right to the surface and we will relive it all over again, causing tension, reactivity and rigidity in our minds and bodies.

The fears of *What if I fail at this? What if they don't back me, or support me, or believe in me?* clouded my thoughts for many years through the transition into doing what I love.

But I kept going. I was being gently nudged every step of the way by God, who was whispering in my ear, *I've got you, keep taking another step, just believe.*

It was hard, but I knew I could not go back to the life I was living before. There was an energy there of intuition that kept driving me forward. That old part of my soul had died. The old beliefs and patterns were still there in my brain, but they more resembled some dying plants in the corner of an unloved room. If I chose to give them fuel, then they would once again flourish and remind me of the old, programmed beliefs that had brought me to my knees not so long ago. I had to keep coming back to my heart, and of course, that meant trust.

Trust the process

Over time, I started to let go. It became my daily practice and constant repetition. I was under the mindset of *Why the fuck not?* It's good to feel good and I wanted like nothing else to start to believe in myself. I woke up with daily affirmations— affirming that I was enough, that I would be kind to my body that day, that I was on the right path, and that I would trust in my journey.

I got high from teaching yoga and movement to those in dark places similar to where I had been. Where as once I looked to get high from stimulants such as coke, sex, shopping and alcohol, it now comes from within and I've learnt to feel the emotions I spent so long numbing and running from. I shared, and still do, many words from my own gurus and teachers that have helped me along the way of learning self-compassion and self-acceptance, and embracing authenticity and goodness. And that feeling of sharing my light was so fucking addictive, it lit me up each time.

So, as the law of attraction goes, what we focus our energy

and attention on is what grows. This of course applies to anything in our environment—what are we choosing to fill our cups with, and the more direct question of how we spend our time and energy.

If you find you are drained, pessimistic or constantly judging and comparing, maybe your environment is not serving you. What can you do? Turn off the TV, use your energy wisely and start to do the things that make you *feel* good. Get outside, have gratitude for *getting* to have today, cuddle your dog, see your friends, connect with other humans, play more, be kind and be the light that you wish to see around you. What you are practising is what will expand around you.

It was over those years of finding my feet that I really started to unravel the layers of myself—and change my environment with people, workplaces, social media feeds and what I chose to do—that my whole life started to become the life I had always dreamed of. A life where I can wake up every day and go 'Holy hell, am I really living a life each day where I can be so grateful and blessed to be in my own skin?'

That was something I *never ever* thought would be possible.

**Ya gotta believe in yourself.
No one else will do it for you.**

Remember that conversation with my father about the same broken record of my life, in which I said: 'I'm doing this for me, not for you. I need to follow my heart. You can choose to support and love me through this or resist it.' My energy of belief started to shine through and my energy of abundance reflected onto those around me. This is how I created a new experience with them. *It had to come from me.*

A lot changed from that moment. I have my dad and my mother to thank immensely for allowing me to step into my light and do what I love.

Not only did I start to heal the relationship with myself, but also with my parents.

To both of my parents here, thank you. I am so grateful for your acceptance, love and guidance. Thank you for allowing me to do what makes my heart happy and for being there no matter what your own beliefs and values may be.

Trusting and allowing, once again, is a practice. If we find ourselves in a state of fear, worry, doubt or anxiety, we have a choice of whether we feed that dragon, or give our energy up to a higher power.

By surrendering the outcome, we take the pressure off and trust that is all working out exactly as it's meant to.

So, let it go?

Yes. Let it go.

Choose to see it differently.

Here is an affirmation you can start to do daily: 'I trust that life is unfolding for me in perfect harmony. I let go of the outcome, I surrender the control and I believe that miracles are coming my way.'

The situation is going to unfold anyway whether you like it or not, so do yourself a favour, call out what you are experiencing in your body—the emotion that is vibrating from your heart—and give it permission to be there. It's OK.

When we do that, the monkey mind settles just enough to give us a moment. We can access the magic of a pause, and the choice to believe another story.

Vibrations deliver us what we ask for

Let's go back to our first story and what happens when we think a thought.

When we think a thought, especially one that is familiar, such as *I'm not smart enough, I am undeserving* or *My body is awful*, we fire and wire the same neurons to strengthen the same synapses that remind us that we are not enough. If we keep giving these neurons attention, the cluster grows and we find it really difficult as we get older to believe any other story about ourselves.

The same applies when we are immersed in feelings of fear, doubt or worry. They envelop us and become us, and before we know it, we have snowballed into a field of negative emotions and feelings, only attracting more of the same.

The more we practise fear-based thoughts, including worry, the more we bring that to our environment. Simply, worry creates more worry.

We *are* what we *think*.

We have created our reality with our words and thoughts.

If we are on a roundabout of the same dialogue—in essence, thinking a thought such as *I'm not enough*—this is backed with emotion. This energy will bring us more of the same.

So if we are constantly running on a low-vibrational energy, then more low-vibe experiences, people, and situations will head our way.

The opposite is also true, hence why I'm SO DAMN PASSIONATE about setting your affirmations, *with emotion*. All the positive thoughts in the world won't shake shit if you don't *believe* them. We need to create a magnet with our emotions and feelings to attract what we want to receive. This is how dreams are created and we can live a life full of abundance in all areas.

Nature is ALWAYS serving. It is here to give back to us. We have been conditioned to 'get in the way'. We try to control outcomes, we try to block things from flowing, we try to resist what is meant to flow. Things get stuck big time and whatever we resist, persists.

Fear, doubt, worry and unworthiness are *not* our natural state. They vibrate at an exceptionally low frequency, and we all know they don't feel so hot.

In contrast, gratitude, kindness, appreciation, excitement and pleasure feel incredible in our being and when we feel them, they light us up, in turn sparking that energy with others. This is our natural state.

I could spend this whole book on energy, as I am a firm believer that our thoughts and words create what we experience. If we want to change our experience, we *must* change our environment.

What I do know is this: if we are on the constant train of fear, doubt, worry, judgement, comparison, self-hate or unworthiness, the practice of those low-vibrational feelings will only generate more of the same. This is what I like to call the roundabout effect. Same shit, different day, and we wonder why five, ten, twenty years later we are still spinning the same story.

I want you to know that at any given moment, your energy, and what you are creating, is up to you. Even in the pandemic that has been a part of our world since 2020, fear surrounds many of us, but you (and I) have a choice not to buy into it, to turn fear to faith, to not give it our attention and choose wisely with how we spend our time, thoughts and conversations, and digest information. If we put that time back into the feel-good moments, and decide to create boundaries around what we talk about, what might happen, what might the future look like? We could choose to go and do something we love, spend time with a person who lights us up, or tune into our creativity and dharma. Maybe, just maybe, we would start to see the changes on a big scale.

I'm not kidding when I say I'm a woman who wants to change the world. Don't ever believe that you can't make a difference. It is entirely up to you, and me, to create what we want to see reflected back to us.

Interrupting the practised patterns

Pausing by breathing allows us to, very briefly, interrupt the pattern of thinking. This is called presence, awareness, being in the moment, so to speak.

We have a choice.

When we feel the pull or fear or the freight train of anxiety, it is then that we need to become present.

Notice your body.

Notice your emotions.

Let it be. It's OK.

Then ask the question: *What is it my heart needs?*

You now have the knowledge to feel empowered about understanding your brain and nervous system and to respond, not react, and shift your energy to feel good.

Shifting your energy

You will realise you can choose to surrender—to become curious, not critical, about why the fear or anxiety is there.

> Let go and let God.
> — Wayne Dyer

By doing this, you will see the fear is there to remind you that you are on the right path. Remember I said it would be uncomfortable, terrifying and unfamiliar. Perfect. This is what we need to grow.

Embrace the fear. Turn your fear into faith, keep your heart open and back the fuck out of what you are doing.

Why? Why not! You may as well. For too long we have played small, thought we couldn't, or thought someone else did it better. You have every right to start to turn your life around. Isn't it time to consider how that might feel?

This book is about you. It is ultimately about being present—paying attention in every moment to your words, your choices, your actions and your thoughts about yourself. I hope that my story can help you understand that we are not alone in our dialogue and our thoughts.

We all struggle. We all battle.

We all feel somewhere along the way that we are not enough.

Remember, the First Noble Truth of Buddhism is that 'all of life is suffering'. It is up to us to choose to find our way back to equanimity, to ride the wave, however messy and however uncomfortable, and find calm within the chaos. Judging a moment, blaming it, resenting it or fighting it takes way too much energy and will sap us of our vitality and lust for life itself.

Be a sitting duck in a messy ocean

As I sit writing this part of the book, I am enjoying an acai bowl from one of my fav Newy cafes. I am beyond excited. I am filled with pride and a have heart full of gratitude, contentment and a sense of achieving something I never thought would be possible: expressing and sharing this story with the intention to give other humans permission to find their own authenticity and love.

I need to highlight the very real struggle that the past four months have been. I have been stretched, pulled and pushed to my edge, financially, mentally and physically. However, I have surrendered and let go every single time. I simply notice the chaos, I notice the darkness, I notice the battles and I notice the anxiety and I choose to sit and ride the (rather huge) waves that are the emotions of the moments. Instead of putting on a brave face, my courage lies within letting go—being vulnerable enough to recognise my pain and suffering for what it is, without trying to change, adapt or mend it. I know that even in these times, I am exactly where I am meant to be.

This means I have been able to stay as present as possible within the mess. I am human, and some days I haven't caught it so quickly, but the very practice of the BE HERE method—especially those first three steps—has helped my body stay in a state of equilibrium and safety amid the storm.

This simple awareness is something that I have now learned. Not so long ago, without presence, I would have been right back on the roundabout. I could have easily reverted back to those old numbing and running patterns and addictive behaviours, and slipped back into the dangerous (and well-practised) dialogue of unworthiness and 'not enough'. The realisation alone of how I have moved through these last four months shows me just how far I have come, and I feel so overwhelmed with love.

I believe in you, but I need *you* to believe in you too, for this is when it all starts to change.

You can shift the energy in the room

When you believe that you are not enough, your energy spills onto those around you—your partner, your workspace, your kids and your environment. It's time to change that belief with practice.

You will start to attract a better relationship or improve the one you are in.

You will learn to say no at work or to friends, and people will respect your decision and you will have more energy.

Your kids will see your shift and start to practise their own authenticity and confidence.

You will wake up with different energy, a vibration of gratitude, kindness and acceptance for yourself.

Repetition is key.

You *must* start to practice self-love now, for you can only love another as much as you love yourself.

YOU ARE NOW HERE

Whatever is unfolding in front of you right now is likely going to unfold anyway. You may as well surrender to it, yield and move through with grace and compassion.

The BE HERE method

I see you, I feel you, and it's OK. What does my HEART need? I'm EMPOWERED with knowledge, and to RESPOND not react, and from here I shift my ENERGY!

Letting in feels like taking a huge weight off your shoulders. Surrender is not giving up: it's giving in and letting be.

Why do we fight so much to hold on to the things that cause us pain? We resist and try to push down the emotions, the feelings, the thoughts and the somatic responses in our body only to create more of the same.

What if we chose to accept the mess as it is, right now,

without the need for more?

How would that feel?

How would your body respond?

I invite you to investigate this for a moment.

In the world we are in, we are conditioned to push on and strive to succeed. We believe that our lives are determined by the number of dollars we have in our bank account, the car we drive and the brand of activewear that we post to our social media account. We think that we need to have a certain number of likes to feel validated and successful.

Can you feel the pressure, just in that paragraph alone? The constant need for more? The belief that when we have this, look like this, achieve this, receive this promotion, live in this suburb, own this house, we will be happy?

We are labelled as many things—a personal trainer, a yoga teacher, a mother, a daughter, a father, a brother, a friend, a sister, a business owner, a wife, a friend, a lover … but it is these labels and pedestals that can separate us in a world that continually makes us feel we are not enough. We are consistently sold products that 'improve' the shape of our butt, our hips and our waist. We concentrate on our financial status, our Instagram followers, our bank accounts and our body types. We feel the need to compare, to judge, to think we are less than or better than others. It's this separation that we are now seeing on a huge scale.

Keep an eye out for The Perfection Pandemic workshops unfolding in some schools across Australia in 2022—all details can be found on my website or Instagram page.

When we can come back to the simple awareness and understanding that we are all one, and not one of us is higher or lower than another, we will find harmony and peace in the world, which ultimately is love. When we feel love, whether it be for ourselves, a pet or a friend, we feel no need to bring down or resent another, as our heart space is full and accepting. It's an energy and it's our natural state.

The layers, the limiting beliefs, the stories and the labels have been learnt along the way. Our job is to recognise when we are being triggered, tune in, dig deep and see what layer we can unravel by asking ourselves the question, *What is it that I'm unwilling to feel?*

Tension will only create more tension. Surrender to what comes up and say thank you, as this will be your biggest teacher in peeling off those layers of judgement, comparison, self-sabotage, unworthiness and the need to perfect or right.

You always have a choice of responding with curiosity (regulated nervous system) or reacting (blocked nervous system).

At any given moment we can choose to change our story and say yes. Be OK with wanting what you want.

Our attention goes to where we focus our energy, negative or positive. That is the law of the Universe. We don't push anything away. What we ask for and believe, we get back to us.

I was always attracting. We always are. I was attracting energy that was lacking. I didn't feel deserving of love or abundance, so of course, it didn't come my way.

It's easy for us to want to change or fix things, or wish they were different. What if we know we are doing the best we can by non-doing? I encourage you to investigate the teachings of the *Tao-te Ching*. Show rather than tell. Do without expectation. Move like water.

To simply see

I want to share with you the essence of freedom. Seeing.

Many of us, including my old self, think we need it all to

succeed in life. The money, the job, the partner, the house, the suburb, the body, the family, the education, the lifestyle … something to be enough.

Some of us question that, sensing that perfection is unattainable. For even when we have it all … we can still have nothing.

For many of us, we are now at wits' end, wondering what this life is all about. Why do we work so hard, how far do we need to push? What does success actually mean?

And the classic … 'What is my purpose?' We all have cargo that we are carrying. They say that if we go through life and do not deliver our cargo, we lead a life of suffering.

Our cargo is not something that we find. It's something we are born with. It's already within us—we just need to peel back the layers.

Death is certain and it looms above all of us. The reality of dying, however, is not so easily understood. Death, I believe, is simply a part of life. It is real, it is part of us, and it could happen tomorrow.

So how are we all living today …?

How do we find peace when the world keeps telling us to keep on doing, striving and perfecting?

We all long to be free. There is a deep sense of longing inside of us that craves self-acceptance, authenticity and honesty, but we are so chained to fear, uncertainty and failure that we are afraid to let go.

We do not realise that it is the mind and the old limiting beliefs that keeps us chained down and searching for more.

In Buddhism, it's about seeing it how it is. Not sugarcoating it; not trying to make it something else; not trying to fix it, change it or manipulate it to fit your programmed mind.

It's about calling it out and being real. Seeing things as they are, not how we want them to be. That is a picture you generate in your mind to hide from the heart.

This, I believe, is true awareness.

I see you, I feel you and it's OK. Let it be.

Suffering is part of life. Embracing it is not what we were taught. Recognising our pain and surrendering to it creates an immense feeling of freedom and acceptance.

Surface changes do not get to the core. Only when we address the source of our problems do we heal their manifestations.

How can I fix them?

If I could offer a forehead-slap emoji here, I would. You cannot ever fix another; we can only 'fix' ourselves.

In my own work I constantly hear from others: 'How do I fix my partner/daughter/friend? They are constantly choosing self-harm and on a path to destruction. I have tried everything in the world to fix them but they are not listening.'

My response is usually this (and originates from a place of love):

> 'I definitely do not know the right answer. I believe none of us know enough to be wrong or right, but what I have learnt is that our energy, our dialogue, our behaviours and our actions are what other people see, and this becomes our teaching to our little ones because they are a sponge that absorbs what unfolds in front of them, especially in those early formative years.

> 'Do you mind if I ask you a question?

> 'How do you feel about your own self-worth? How

do you see yourself in the mirror? How do you show up on your social media feed? Do you love the person you see?'

This is deep and probably somewhat uncomfortable, but my intention is just to spark the thought, *Maybe if I offered myself more kindness, I would experience more gratitude and that energy would reflect out to my loved ones.*

I get it. It's confronting, challenging and hard to hear, but if we are trying to change someone else, the best we can do is be a light of our own. If we are judging ourselves in the mirror, if we are complaining about the width of or cellulite on our thighs, if we are comparing ourselves to other people on our socials, then that energy will be picked up and put into action by those around us. Monkey see, monkey do.

Simply choosing to say thank you each day when we wake up and look in the mirror and use the dialogue of *God I freaking love you today and think you are amazing* instead of *I wish my tummy would disappear* changes the ball game. You shift the vibration and the energy (and your world) starts to change. And the best bit? Your kids get to experience that too!

The Perfection Pandemic

It is worth noting here how we show up on our *socials*. This is the essence and backbone of my second book and workshop series The Perfection Pandemic.

The images and videos on our social media feed are a guide for how our kids and teens show up on theirs. If we are using a filter or body editor on nearly every photo, then how can we possibly deliver a message that we are enough as we are?

Our kids see our feeds, and they also see how we try to look and how we post the best angle or view of ourselves, touch up our wrinkles, eliminate pores or trim our waist.

This next sentence is absolutely not from a place of judgement, but I will say it as it is: This is dangerous, addictive and not our way forward if we want to raise kids that are comfortable in their own skin, accepting of their bodies and confident enough to speak their truth and be authentic.

The rise of sexualisation in kids on apps such as TikTok, Snapchat and OnlyFans is gaining so much momentum; our kids are seeing images of perfect, filtered and edited faces and bodies. Of course, if this is what they are constantly seeing, this is what they will believe to be true.

How to change it? It's up to you, and your journey back to love. If you feel love for yourself, I guarantee you there is no need to alter your image, compare yourself to another, or judge your body against the next influencer you see. You are completely content with where you are at and have no need to edit, modify or change it. Your kids have the permission to follow suit.

If we come from a place of surrender, we learn to appreciate the 'isness' of where we are at—body, environment, job, financial status and what we own. When we learn to have gratitude for what we do have rather than what we don't, our energy is that of showing up and it is contagious. Everyone around you will feel your contentment, your appreciation and your love.

Let go and let God

If someone you love is in immense suffering, surrender it up to God. Ask and pray for guidance and hand it over. It's a big enough job doing the work for ourselves, let alone trying to do the work for another. Leave it up to the big guns and trust that it is now in the hands of the Universe.

This is where humility and surrender, two of the essential teachings of the *Tao-te Ching*, come into play. Do what you can with a whole heart and then place that person you care about in the hands of God/Universe/Divine Spirit.

It's working out exactly as it's meant to.

Let go of the wheel.

For true surrender, we need to let go of trying to fix, manipulate or amend. We need to let go of wanting things to be different from what is here right now. We need to surrender the pain and trauma of the past—the limiting beliefs that hold us back because we don't feel enough due to something that happened in our childhood.

We need to let go of the label we have carried for so long that thinks we are undeserving of love and compassion. I guarantee you that wherever that story has emerged from, it is most definitely not true for you anymore.

We need to yield to what is here right now without the need for more. The body we have at the moment is perfect how it is. It is what we do from this moment that matters. Judging it, comparing it, blaming others for the state of it and not taking ownership isn't doing anything for us.

Accept it. Acknowledge it and practise loving it. Why not? You have the choice to feel good, to feel alive, to feel gratitude and acceptance.

Gratitude is the highest vibration you will ever have. If you are not doing so already, start each day with your affirmations and the practice of gratitude. Ultimately, this is key for watching your new life unfold.

But it must be practised and on repeat like your favourite song.

But I'm scared! I don't know how to be authentic

You do, I promise. It's always been there, but it's covered up with fear and the feeling of being judged or not accepted. Possibly some people wouldn't like to see you deciding to step into your highest self.

So what about all the fear I'm feeling?

This is your key to show up. Fear presents when we are moving through new waters. It's challenging, it's rough, it's super uncomfortable. Great.

Go there. Step outside the box of comfort! Use your fear to remind you to turn back to faith. Trust that you are exactly where you need to be. You can only grow from new experiences and, as humans, that is exactly what we are here to do.

Instead of allowing ourselves to be overcome by the fear—and this is especially relevant to what we are seeing going on in 2022—can we possibly choose to see things differently? It's easy to see how the media can keep us living in fear so that we buy the products, do the thing and follow along, as fear is the biggest driver in selling anything to the masses. Being aware is key, that's all. It's not wrong, it's not right, it just is and it's the world we live in.

As you know, my experience of working in the media opened my eyes. I keep an open mind and am not immune to the techniques used to get people to believe a headline.

We have to remember that we always have a choice. I encourage you to be curious about your body being your teacher. Stress is a leading cause of inflammation and sickness in the body and it is also something that with presence, we can do something about—which in my eyes, is so empowering.

The big lesson of surrender

We are in a world that's constantly changing, so let's let go of the control.

These last few words remind me to come back to my own heart. I wrote this last story in Nelson Bay, New South Wales after taking an impromptu weekend away while all of Sydney was shut down with the pandemic. It felt the right time to get these last words out.

As I was driving there, my body started to tingle, buzz, feel emotion and feel incredibly lit. I had to pull over at one point as I had tears streaming down my face. My nan and family have a huge connection with Anna Bay, and as I was moving through the area, I felt Nan's presence fully.

I dedicate this book to a woman that changed my life forever, my nan, Nancy Linton. A magical soul who held on to her own pain and trauma for nearly seventy years—only for it to come out in her later years.

We can only forgive ourselves if we have the tools to do so. For many of us, if we are not aware how to unblock and release these past events, we reach the end of our days holding on to events, situations, experiences and regrets that were many moons ago.

Nan, you were a fighter, a giver, an amazing mother to your sons, and a grandmother to four beautiful granddaughters. We were so damn lucky to have you. You were a woman that shared so much love to others, and you delivered the ultimate gift and message to me: to follow my heart, to keep dreaming, to never stifle my imagination, to defy the odds and to stoke the fire in my belly that equated to love and compassion.

On rare occasions in those later years, when we spent time together, I would walk into her room at the nursing home and she would light up. Her body would open and she would say these words often: 'How are you so happy? You are glowing … what is your secret?'

I would tell her that I just love what I'm doing, sharing yoga, teaching workshops to teens on body image and self-talk, and facilitating movement classes.

She would then lose the smile, and the old familiar dialogue of 'Oh, you can never make a living out of that' would creep back in. The energy would change, and we would go back to talking about the weather, the food in the nursing home, and the man down the hallway who kept shitting his pants as he had lost control of his bowels.

The small talk never gets you anywhere.

At first, when these words were said, I felt offended, upset and small. I then chose to use this to my benefit and was like, you know what, I'm doing the thing that not many people get a chance to do.

So, thank you, Nan. Thank you for showing me the way forward to follow my heart, chase my dreams, and step into my full, imperfect, playful and authentic self.

Nan taught me to surrender and let go. It's not worth my energy to hold on to the guilt, blame or shame that has presented itself in my past. Now is the only moment that matters.

We experienced Nan in her final years of life in the nursing home. She was gripping for sanity. As mentioned in Story Two, she would write the words *Help me* on the walls. She was in so much pain. There were conversations that broke my heart with her expression of the words, 'I've been such a horrible person. I can never forgive myself.' These words were with her on her final day, just before her birthday in December, when her tension, the stuck emotions and the blocked trauma were like a demon inside her.

She battled for more than eight hours. She pushed us away, she resisted the morphine and help. She screamed, getting up and out of her chair and back down. The energy of these last moments was intense and fear driven—my parents and I will never forget it.

Yet there were moments where she surrendered and her whole body yielded to what was, if only for a moment before the rigidity, the old patterns and the pain of the past haunted her thoughts.

Nan, you will always be my biggest teacher to let go, surrender and not hold on. I will be forever grateful.

This is where this book reaches its crescendo. Surrender it up and let it go: the stories, the limiting beliefs, the idea that we are not enough, the things we have done, the things we have said, and the ups and downs along the way.

Yielding and letting yourself experience your emotions, rather than fighting them your whole life, will reward you with energy, acceptance and, above all, yourself.

Trauma that has not been felt or forgiven will stay in our body and drive our thoughts, emotions, behaviours and actions until we allow ourselves to feel to heal, forgive, let go, and embrace who we are, imperfections and all.

The energy that was stuck with Nan was lifelong pain. Most of the time she skimmed above the surface, but like a river, we cannot block the flow of water, and one day it will overflow. This dear soul never had the tools or allowed herself to forgive herself for something that society had deemed 'not OK'.

What's not OK is human beings holding on to pain and trauma that is now in our past. What's not OK is spending the rest of our lives with shitty dialogue with ourselves for a story that we created out of other people's expectations and views. How we think we should be.

That's what this book is all about, and the BE HERE method.

The BE HERE method and the Watch YA Language six-week immersions and courses run online, in schools and for corporate and school groups across Australia. It is my heart and soul to share this—especially in schools so that we can prevent things such as full-blown eating disorders, depression and suicides by having the tools to know that with practice we can always choose love over fear.

As I near the end of this book, I feel so much love. Love for myself that I never knew was available, contentment that I had only dreamed of, and acceptance that I thought was found in the external world. I spent years searching for all of this in the 'things'—the body, the job, the partner, the career, the salary, the goals, the weight, the social media status, the clothes, the car, the house and the labels.

It was here the whole time. I just had to go inside. This is the same for you ... we just have to unravel the layers. You do not need to find your purpose (your dharma); it has already found you.

None of those 'things' matter. It's important to have them, but attachment to the external will have us feeling a sense of lack, wishing and wanting for more, and wanting to be better than ...

Here is where it's at. This is what I know: all we have is now. This is it.

So there is no better time than now to watch ya language. Be the light you wish to be for others.

With a beginner mind, you are able to see people, workplaces, loved ones and—most importantly—yourself from a new and curious point of view. It took me nearly thirty years to do this but I'm so grateful for the practice of presence, which was able to bring me back to the self who had been craving my attention all those years. This is the practice of seeing.

I now accept who I am without the need for more. My heart is full. I need no one and no thing to complete me. Growth comes from being the student always and knowing that you are always open to learning. I could die tomorrow and be so grateful for every single messy step along the way. I have learnt to shift my fear and comparison to curiosity and awareness that there is something great I am going to learn here.

It is said you can only love another as much as you love yourself. I now know this book has allowed me to do that fully.

I will not lie when I say I was triggered by my own book. I was confronted with stories and limiting beliefs that I had to face before completion of this book. I dare say, through life, there will be many more.

Bring it on, I say.

Move forward with love

As I finish this book in March 2022, I am reminded of the journey of surrender and trust that I chose to take; I had no idea where it would lead, but in these final pages I see so clearly what God had planned. It could not be rushed, it could not be hurried. It had to come through me in divine time.

I close my eyes here and gently pray a silent thank you. I'm fully ready for whatever this next roller-coaster may bring, and I'm beyond excited for the growth, the challenges and the messiness that life will continue to offer.

That chapter is now done. Over. Three and a half years of putting words on pages, rolling through the stories, and sitting with the lessons and the work that I needed to do to process the emotions. I am ready. Ready to fully receive whatever may be next and dive in full throttle with my heart and soul.

My heart is now fully open and ready to share this *Watch YA Language* journey with the world, wherever that takes me. I have never felt so content, curious, open, in love and accepting in my life as what I do sharing these last few words. It took time and it will always take work.

My hope is that by diving in and doing the work ourselves, we can reach a level of understanding of our past without judging or comparing it. Then we can own it, have compassion for it and gain true awareness around why our dialogue is what it is. Then, we can do something about it. This is possible at any age; you just have to *believe* you can. And you now have the tools of the BE HERE method to do so!

We never have our shit together. Life would be pretty boring if that were the case.

Who knows where this journey of love and acceptance may lead. But I'm ready for the ride.

My hope is that you are ready too.

Get excited about what is about to unfold for you, because when you start to watch ya language, your whole world will change; you will experience gratitude and love on a level you never thought possible ... and what a gift that will be to share with your loved ones.

Now, go and create your new story ... one that stems from love.

Megs x

THE STATEMENT

GET CLEAR ON WHAT YOU WANT
Imagine and dream in desire of
what it would feel like.

I believe that anything is possible. I am creating a life
sharing my blessings to others.
I know that if I stay true to my heart, abundance in all
forms is available to me.

I choose to give and share what I have learned, and still
learning, to others every day. I promise to be open, fluid and
always a practitioner.

My body deserves absolute and unconditional love, respect
and compassion daily. My desire to feel good grows every day.
I know that when I feel good, more comes back to me, lights
me up and those around.

I am worthy of all I desire. I release doubt. I let go of
tension, and I choose to turn fear to faith. I surrender to the
unknown path, and I TRUST THE PROCESS.

I am supported, loved, enough, and worthy of it all.

Thank you, I am so grateful for my body, this day, and the
ability to give back and serve.

RESOURCES

For more of Megs!
Meg Linton, Watch YA Language
Website: www.watchyalanguage.com
Instagram: @watch.ya.language
YouTube: Meg Linton
Online courses, school presentations and coaching accessible through the website.

Millie Thomas, Eating Disorder Recovery Coach and Podcast
@millietnz
Beyond Blue @beyondblueofficial
EndED Australia @endedaustralia
Dr Kirsty Seward, Body Image Coach and Behavioural Scientist
@drkirstyseward
Cathy Feenan, Life Empowerment Coach @cathy_feenan_

Books that have helped me understand the mind/body connection
Siegel, D., 2011. *Mindsight*. New York: Oneworld Publications.
Dispenza, D., 2014. *You Are the Placebo*. Hay House Publishing.
Bernstein, G., 2016. *The Universe Has Your Back*. Hay House.
Hay, L., 1999. *You Can Heal Your Life Gift*. Hay House Publishing.
DANA, D., 2018. *Polyvagal theory in therapy*. W W NORTON.
Siegel, D. and Bryson, T., n.d. *The power of showing up*.

When you are ready to dive in, the universe will show you the way. You are now here. Your choice to now put this time and energy back into you, will not just start to heal you, but those around you by deciding to do the work. From my heart to yours, thank you.

AFFIRMATIONS

I choose to be kind to my body and soul today.

I am here now. What a gift to be here today.

I choose to be curious not critical about what unfolds today.

I trust the process, surrender to the guidance of God today.

My body deserves my love, attention and kindness today.

I am thankful for waking up today. I get to have today.

I choose to speak to myself with love today.

I choose to feel good today!

I am choosing to live today in absolute gratitude.

I let go. I surrender and I trust the process.

I am worthy. This was always the story.

When I am quiet, I am able to hear.

I am open to receive the love that I deserve.

My choice to show up empowers my child to do the same.

I am working on setting clear boundaries for myself and my self-care.

When I set boundaries, I am showing up and open to receive more love.

I am the creator of my experiences. I choose to have fun with this today.

I choose to believe that this _____ is possible today and am open to being guided without force.

When I receive love, I can give love. My cup must be filled first.

ABOUT THE AUTHOR

Meg Linton is a woman determined to change the world.

After struggling through nearly three decades of disordered eating, poor mental health and low self-esteem, Meg decided it was time to face her fears and start living the life she wanted and deserved.

Meg now visits schools and businesses across Australia, teaching the BE HERE method that enabled her to reclaim her self-esteem, freedom and future. She is a firm believer that the way we speak to ourselves determines our experience of life.

In her first book, *Watch YA Language*, Meg shares tips and tools for working through trauma, practising self-compassion, and passing on these vital life skills to the next generation.

CPSIA information can be obtained
at www.ICGtesting.com
Printed in the USA
LVHW041313020622
720142LV00004B/132

9 780645 262636